Praise for *Everywhere Holy*

"This beautifully written book will give you eyes to see the God hiding in plain sight in your right-now life. If your life has felt too busy or complicated for God, Kara will gently take you by the hand and help trace the sacredness of your days as they stand right now. Her words will restore souls."

—SARAH BESSEY, AUTHOR OF *MIRACLES AND OTHER REASONABLE THINGS* AND *JESUS FEMINIST*

"In our hurried, overly-connected, under-nurtured culture, we need easily accessible, grace-filled forms of refuge. Places we can show up late, messy, scared, and imperfect, yet still be seen, restored, and encouraged. With relatable truths and exquisite insights, Kara Lawler invites us to discover just how close we are to the peace, promise, and fulfillment of God. If you're feeling weary, worried, or plain worn out—look no further. *Everywhere Holy* is your guidebook to finding real hope, relatable faith, and therapeutic peace."

—RACHEL MACY STAFFORD, *NEW YORK TIMES* BESTSELLING AUTHOR OF *HANDS FREE MAMA, HANDS FREE LIFE,* AND *ONLY LOVE TODAY*

"From the moment I opened *Everywhere Holy*, Kara Lawler's exquisite stories made me breathe easier, lighter, and more rhythmically. Reading her reflections, I felt time stopping and my soul being nourished with each story. In our culture of busy and disconnect from our own hearts, one another, and nature, Kara invites us into her home, onto her land, and into moments of exhale, connection, and slowing down to feel the pulse of the Holy in our lives. Kara genuinely shares with us her struggles—within her own heart and relationships—and her grace-filled moments of peace and connection. In doing so, readers will find themselves feeling less alone, more hopeful, and better able to see and experience it all as holy. Our world is hungry for such experiences of the divine and remembering that it's all holy. Kara gently takes our hand and leads right here into the holy."

—LISA McCROHAN, MA, LCSW-C, SOMATIC EXPERIENCING PSYCHOTHERAPIST AND AUTHOR OF *GEMS OF DELIGHT*

"In *Everywhere Holy*, Kara Lawler reminds us of the beauty that surrounds us every day, when we dare to live with eyes wide open. As we honor the sacred around us, we find more of what our hearts long for, and see that God has been with us each moment and step of the journey."

—JAMIE C. MARTIN, AUTHOR OF *INTROVERTED MOM: YOUR GUIDE TO MORE CALM, LESS GUILT, AND QUIET JOY*

"I have read and admired Kara Lawler's writing for years, but she takes it to a whole new level in *Everywhere Holy*. Lawler's words are both thought-provoking and soul-quenching. Her eloquent illustrations of finding the divine in the every day leads readers on a quest to be inspired and awestruck by their own journeys. I didn't want to put this book down! *Everywhere Holy* will be a blessing to all those who read it."

—ASHLEY WILLIS, AUTHOR OF *THE NAKED MARRIAGE*

"*Everywhere Holy* is the tangible reminder that we were created to look for God in all the places. So often, we get caught up in this busy life that we forget to stop and look for his presence, experience his creation, and remember that he longs to be with us in the simple and mundane. Kara's beautiful craft of storytelling brought me to so many intimate moments of her life and compelled me to look for God in my own, so that I, too, could live a life saturated in his holiness."

—LAUREN EBERSPACHER, AUTHOR OF *MIDNIGHT LULLABIES* AND THE *FROM BLACKTOP TO DIRT ROAD* BLOG

"In a world of confusion and disarray, *Everywhere Holy* offers a space of refuge and recovery for the weary soul. Kara calls us deeper into the beauty of a Father who abundantly surrounds us. With beautiful storytelling, we begin to uncover the wonder of what we so often miss."

—KELLY BALARIE, SPEAKER, BLOGGER
AT *PURPOSEFUL FAITH*, AND AUTHOR OF
FEAR FIGHTING AND *BATTLE READY*

"To open *Everywhere Holy* is to enter a world of quiet wonder, shimmering beauty, and deep growth. Kara Lawler invites us to see the ordinary—work, family, home, nature—with fresh eyes, eager to grasp the holy waiting in every moment. This book is a gift of gratitude and grace."

—LAURA KELLY FANUCCI, AUTHOR OF *EVERYDAY*
SACRAMENT: THE MESSY GRACE OF PARENTING

"In *Everywhere Holy*, Kara's writing is more poetic and her graceful notes on the pages come out more like a melody than words. Her love of language and seeing things differently has shifted my perspective to notice. And the noticings are the notes that continue to draw me in, story after story in this book. You have just been given the gift of all gifts—to sit and listen while Kara shares words that flow like songs that will tune your heart for more. The way Kara brings her children into the life she shares with us in these pages is how I want to draw my children close as we see God together. Kara reminds us to find holiness right here, right now. And holy can be everywhere we look for it if we grab hold of it and don't let it out of our sight. This book will give you the awe-filled path to find it."

—BLYTHE DANIEL, LITERARY AGENT AND
AUTHOR OF *MENDED: RESTORING THE*
HEARTS OF MOTHERS AND DAUGHTERS

"To be human is to be ever searching for the antidote to our loneliness, the fulfillment of our yearnings, and the satiation of hungers we often don't even fully understand. In this beautifully written book, Kara Lawler takes us each by the hand and teaches us how to find God in every moment and place and in doing so, leads us tenderly to the only stream that will ever quench our thirst."

—HALLIE LORD, SIRIUSXM RADIO HOST AND
AUTHOR OF ON THE OTHER SIDE OF FEAR

Everywhere Holy

Seeing Beauty,
Remembering Your
Identity, and Finding God
Right Where You Are

KARA LAWLER

NELSON
BOOKS

An Imprint of Thomas Nelson

Published in Nashville, Tennessee, by Nelson Books, an imprint of Thomas Nelson. Nelson Books and Thomas Nelson are registered trademarks of HarperCollins Christian Publishing, Inc.

Material excerpted from *The Book of Awakening* © 2000 by Mark Nepo used with permission from Red Wheel Weiser, LLC Newburyport, MA, www.redwheelweiser.com.

Thomas Nelson titles may be purchased in bulk for educational, business, fund-raising, or sales promotional use. For information, please e-mail SpecialMarkets@ThomasNelson.com.

Scripture quotations are taken from THE MESSAGE, copyright © 1993, 2002, 2018 by Eugene H. Peterson.

Any Internet addresses, phone numbers, or company or product information printed in this book are offered as a resource and are not intended in any way to be or to imply an endorsement by Thomas Nelson, nor does Thomas Nelson vouch for the existence, content, or services of these sites, phone numbers, companies, or products beyond the life of this book.

ISBN 978-1-4002-1164-7 (eBook)
ISBN 978-1-4002-1163-0 (TP)

Library of Congress Control Number: 2019947791

Printed in the United States of America
19 20 21 22 23 LSC 10 9 8 7 6 5 4 3 2 1

For my children, who
helped me remember.

"If I really wanted to pray I'll tell you what I'd do. I'd go out into a great big field all alone or into the deep, deep woods, and I'd look up into the sky—up—up—up—into that lovely blue sky that looks as if there was no end to its blueness. And then I'd just *feel* a prayer."

—LUCY MAUD MONTGOMERY,
ANNE OF GREEN GABLES

Contents

Introduction: A Thousand Windows   xi

Chapter 1.   The Fog Rises   1
Chapter 2.   Oh, the Rainbows in the Sky   13
Chapter 3.   Spirit on the Move   26
Chapter 4.   Right Here, Right Where I'm to Be   41
Chapter 5.   They, So Fresh from God   51
Chapter 6.   Snow on Daffodils   66
Chapter 7.   Walk with Me   81
Chapter 8.   This Beating, Tattered Heart   94
Chapter 9.   Small Prayers   111
Chapter 10.   And the Rain Falls   125
Chapter 11.   Angels on Guard   140
Chapter 12.   The World Within   152
Chapter 13.   Life Less Difficult   168
Chapter 14.   A Language Without Words   177
Chapter 15.   Me, Just the Same   193

Epilogue: Wild, Holy Ground   197
Acknowledgments   201
Notes   205
About the Author   207

Introduction

A Thousand Windows

Oh, these vast, calm, measureless mountain days . . .
Days in whose light everything seems equally divine,
opening a thousand windows to show us God.

—JOHN MUIR, *MY FIRST*
SUMMER IN THE SIERRA

When I was a little girl, I felt God's presence when I was in nature, especially at my childhood home in the Allegheny Mountains of Pennsylvania in the Appalachian mountain range. My favorite spot was the clearing in the woods behind our house. I haven't been to the clearing in over two decades, but in my memory, it is wild, magical, all moss-covered rock and glittering light. The ground and the mountains surrounding it, with their peaks and valleys, were where I belonged. Like Anne of Green Gables said in my favorite childhood book, "I'd look up into the sky—up—up—up . . . and then I'd just *feel* a prayer."[1] My soul was home. But as it is in life, I grew and changed, my parents and I moved, and I dreamed bigger. I eventually forgot the clearing, the filtered light, and what it felt like to be there.

Years later, as a college student studying abroad in England, I visited Salisbury Cathedral and was struck by how strongly I felt God there. It was the first time I had ever been in a cathedral like it, so I spent some time alone in silence, kneeling in supplication. God was there; I knew it. I was only twenty years old and his whisper was there, his window was there, and I was afraid I wouldn't hear it or see it again if I left. I have never told anyone about that day because the holiness there seemed almost *too* holy to talk about; it seemed unreal. I had felt God in that church as I had in nature, but I hadn't considered that I could meet him everywhere and anywhere if I'd only look. And never did I consider that holy moments were occurring in my everyday life. I didn't yet know that the art of noticing beauty is a spiritual discipline—the best form of prayer I've found yet, the best way to find gratitude—and that life, in and of itself, is holy.

I recently had lunch with a friend I hadn't seen in a while, and she asked me how I knew if I was doing "the right thing." I confessed that *most days, I don't know.* Many days, I'm pretty unsure. In the midst of the ordinary or in times of struggle, I think we all sometimes ask ourselves, *What does it mean to* feel *good enough, whole enough, holy enough,* right where I am? *How can I even find beauty and honor it when my life feels so heavy?* After very full days, we sometimes feel exhausted; many words are left unspoken; many things are left undone. We feel like we have messed up, misstepped, misspoken, fallen, but in the midst of it all, we want to feel grateful for what we have and the blessings that surround us. At the end of the day, we want to know how to focus on what lifts us up instead of all that weighs us down.

Looking for holiness all around and seeing that as a form of prayer has helped me. I invite you to join me, wherever or whoever you are, as we discover how to see *holy* everywhere, right in our own lives. I'll share stories that have helped me see more holy in my own life; may they help you notice the same in yours. I believe that it is in giving recognition to our lives that we offer up one of the greatest forms of prayer. And as a result, I really think you'll see your identity coming into focus, the realization of how you're to work in the world, in all the ways I have. For me, this journey of identity has been one of self-acceptance, of me *as I am* and of the Spirit gifts I've been given.

I offer this piece of my heart, this book, to you with the hope that you'll find yourself in these pages too. This book is for those who find themselves stumbling and faltering and even sometimes downright falling, facedown, right in the muck of a mud puddle on a rocky mountain trail. It's for the one still in the mud and it's for the one who has picked herself up, all muddied face and dirtied hair, and continued her walk, searching for that divine light. It's for the one who has lent a hand, dirtying her own clothes to help the one who fell. It is for me. It is for *you*.

While I do share my own stories here, I'm absolutely no expert; *I'm a work in progress* and this is a story of my own journey. This is an *I share with you, and we learn together* type of book. We *see* better together. This is not a posture or a prescription, and I'm not a theologian. I'm a wife, mother, teacher, and writer, and I'm writing at my desk in my country house on the hill by the wood's edge, surrounded by my people and animals. My desk has a view of the fields and all the hay is baled this time of year. That's where I am.

Last year, right before I submitted title ideas for this book, Matt, my son, then age nine, said to me, "Hey Mom, you can find God everywhere you are." *Finally*, I know that to be true. God's windows are all around. It is my hope that we can do this together and you see God right where *you* are—right in the college classroom, if that's where you are, or in your office at work, or on the bus. I hope you can see the holiness right in the bathroom as you bathe an old dog or a new, chubby baby, right in the garden as you tend to the tomatoes or the hydrangea, right in the city as you walk down a crowded street. That very perspective has helped me remember my own identity again and see the beauty and the holiness in this life.

Let's journey together, crossing mountains and walking through valleys with the sun on our faces, although I can't always promise bright skies. We're sure to encounter some rocky terrain and rainy weather, but when the sun shines in the clearing, all flitting and perfect, windows of divine light, we'll be all the more grateful. The path won't always be straight or smooth and we might stumble, but it's a journey worth taking. God's there, watching. Holy is there, waiting.

CHAPTER 1

The Fog Rises

Memory's fog is rising.

—EMILY DICKINSON

When life feels heavy, sometimes it's hard to remember that eventually the fog rises and lifts over the mountains. I never paid much attention to the patterns of the fog until I embarked on what would become a life-changing and horrible bout with anxiety and depression that ultimately became a true reckoning in a coming-to-Jesus moment. It was a bending of the knee, a breaking of will that finally resulted in various forms of help, yet as hard as it was, in it I found the power of pain, recovery, and the promise of the sun peeking through the fog.

One day, when I was practicing one of my very favorite stilling practices to escape my own mind—walking through the fields across from our house—I prayed as I walked and begged for help, the fog only just lifting away from the grass. At one point, I felt a brief peace wash over me and a thought crossed my mind: *the fog always rises.* With those words, I have embraced how to live, despite the fact that I can't control everything, especially the lifting of the fog and the eventual revelation of the sun. It seems simple, but so many of us try to control things that are simply beyond our control. Struggles actually can advance us on the path of seeing beauty again and finding God and, for me, discovering who I *really* am. Like the birds I listen to every morning, I have learned to sing, even during the difficult times. Sometimes, it's by walking into that very mist that we grow in ways we never would have otherwise. Sometimes, it's through what becomes the fog's reprieve that we can appreciate the blaze of the sun.

A few years ago, in the depths of this struggle, there was only one place I wanted to go: to my childhood home and to the clearing behind it, wondering if the clearing was still the way I remembered it. My parents sold the house in 1996, but that didn't stop me from driving the forty-five minutes from where I live with my own family now to the dirt road that house sits on and walking on the road in front of the house. My dream was to get to the clearing tucked back behind the house. I wondered what the clearing would look like to me, at that time, a woman in her late thirties.

I went to the back road by my old house whenever the opportunity presented itself, often even unexpected to me, and I walked up and down the road, stopping to pick up decaying black walnuts in green casings—"stink bombs" we used to call them. I marveled at the total silence, the memory of what it was to be a kid enshrouded by trees, and as I walked, I questioned if this was the place I could find myself: *What is missing from my life? Maybe I can find God on this road, by this small creek, meeting me on these walks if I only allow him? Maybe I can get to the clearing again, if I could only gain the courage to? Maybe I can find myself? Maybe I can remember who I once was?* And that's what my walks became on those late summer days that turned into the frigid days of November—a place to meet God, a place I felt just a little bit okay, a place I could catch my breath, a place I could remember who I once was, a place that seemed to whisper, "Yes, this is holy enough. I'll meet you here." And God did meet me there, amid the dusty air of the breeze.

After these visits to the road by my old house, I would return, saying a prayer that I could be the mother my children deserved and would be able to get it together enough until they were fast asleep. Intermittently, I'd get relief. One day, after a horrible three weeks, I found myself singing, something I love to do and something my children have come to expect from me. I was singing and Matt smiled at me, surprised to hear it. When I saw his surprise and realized the sound was coming from my own mouth, I smiled back. And I knew, despite what happened, that I'd be okay.

The song, coupled with the smile, was a brief reprieve from heartbreaking worry and soul-crushing fear. It was the confirmation that I could carry on—just like you, no matter what you are facing.

One day, I was walking outside with my daughter, Maggie, by then two, and realized I was able to focus on her for the first time in over a month. At first, I was sad and started to berate myself with thoughts of all I hadn't done, hadn't noticed, hadn't been able to be, but then I just stood and stared at her, committed to notice now. Her ringlets had gotten longer and now fell past her shoulders. *How? When? How hadn't I noticed?* When she held up a purple flower, the lavender of the flower complemented the hint of lavender in her blue eyes. She looks so pretty in purple, one of my most favorite colors to see. I knew it was confirmation of my calling to be her mother—to notice color, to breathe in the faces of my children like air. I tucked the flower in her hair, and she smiled at me and said, "Mommy, do you want to run?" She took off, her suddenly long curls bouncing as she ran. I chased her up the mountain, watching her curls against the backdrop of all the lush green of a fall not yet upon us.

Recently, I was with Matt at bedtime. He's used to me being around as he drifts to sleep, and despite the fact that he is nine now and growing—all leggy, jawline appearing—he usually still wants me to lie down with him for a little bit each night. It has become a bit of a ritual, really, and each night, he tells me about his day, his triumphs, his worries, his insecurities, his pride. He talks and tells me he can't sleep unless he does, so I listen, and after talking to me, he hugs me and closes his eyes. Often, I fall asleep myself because with him, I feel a calm I don't feel around others. Next to him, I am quieted to a peace sleep actually can't duplicate, recreate, or master. It's the power of the *still*, really, the knowledge that I was chosen for this life, right there in the dark, right with the small boy beside me.

That night, as the stillness and warmth of the room overtook me, Matt said to me, "Mom, sometimes small thoughts well up inside of me until I feel like I'm going to burst. Even one can take up so much room. That's why I like talking to you each night. Then there's more room." I pulled him to me, kissed his forehead, and told him what a great explanation that really was. *I'm just like that, after all.* He seemed content with that, his worries of the day disappearing into sleep. I'm lucky to be the person he can tell all to, the person he knows won't judge him but will always help him. I'm his *enough* space. Maybe it will help for you to think about your enough space. Who is a way *through* for you? Who are *you* a way through for? Who helps you to make more room? In me, Matt sees a way through, and I know a lot about how important the way through is. He's a way through for me too.

In the still of the mornings at our house, the fog lifts from the mountains in the most beautiful display, somber and holy. It's quiet as it rises and drifts over the mountains, the yard, my driveway. It looks like a blanket, covering the earth and the mountains, and I try to see it for what it is: here, now, part of the morning, just like the anxiety is a part of me, part of *who I am now*. Yes, anxiety is like the fog, and like the mountain, I'm always waiting for it to lift and the sun to shine but doing my best to see the beauty it has shown, the blanket of it like the arms of my husband, the small-child hands in mine, the peace that comes with prayer.

The fog of one particular morning was thick and mimicked the anxiety that followed me. Both anxiety and depression can feel that way to me—like sunglasses after you've left the cold of a movie theater and head back into the summer sun and warmth outside the theater walls. Your glasses steam up and you can't see well; you can't see anything, really, and it's so disorienting. You know the sun is there and a small hand is in yours, but the sunglasses—the fog on them—prevents you from truly enjoying any of it. Life is so distorted, and even faces are harder to see; lights are the hardest, but it's the light you crave—such a dichotomous conflict, a walking oxymoron. Anxiety and depression are both like that—trying hard to see through a haze, the thickness of air sometimes makes it hard to catch your breath, the way the humidity felt that summer I went to Texas with a friend. Do you know the humidity that makes you catch your breath? We spent a few days in Texas and I still replay it as some of the best times I've spent with a friend.

That was before anxiety held my hand, all day every day. I'd try to let go and when I'd finally wrangle my hand free, it would hug me without permission. Actually, both anxiety and depression often feel like trespassers walking on posted land—land I'd claimed as mine, but they ignored the posted signs. It felt like a defeat at first, but it wasn't that. The acceptance of them, the quiet acceptance of them as *who I am now* is one of my greatest victories. While I hope they leave me someday, I'm trying hard to focus on the gifts that have been revealed in their visit. The fog has become a symbol to me, the mist rising from the mountains, the sunshine that comes—eventually. I've learned that the fog will lift if we just keep walking.

The sun sinks low at our house nightly. The sun fades all around but has one final show, one final display of absolute glory, a light show of pinks and oranges, purples and blues, right before the darkness falls, the owl hoots, and the coyotes howl. I love this final show almost as much as I love the sunrise, something I never even knew I loved until I became a mother and was up earlier than I ever thought I should, could, or would be. Then the sunrise was a respite from the night—the crying baby, the night that seemed to mock me with its murmuring of sleep. Then, when the sun rose, I was relieved and poured a cup of coffee. The hot coffee and the light became my prayer (and *are*, even still, even now)—the sun rising became the symbol that I, too, could and would endure another day. The sun, confident in her approach, helped me be confident in mine.

I once dreaded the night, but now those days are behind me, and I've learned the true reward of the darkness and the night in its literal and metaphorical sense. One of those nights, when Maggie was a baby and I was struggling with postpartum depression, I found myself crying out, tears streaming down my face: "*Please* help *me!*" I petitioned, but a crying Maggie was awake, again, rousing her brother too. I was alone at home with both kids because my husband, Mike, worked some nights back then. Desperate, I gathered her in my arms and Matt crawled into bed with me and we all fell into a deep sleep, an answered prayer, a petition signed, a plea heard.

When we all woke, I thought of answered prayers from screaming pleas. Darkness is like that now to me—holy and true. The night comes but it has its own rewards, its own moments of curling up under a crocheted blanket my Meemom made, and resting, its own moments of peace amid discomfort. I've seen the rewards of the darkness and the gifts of the night. The night isn't so scary anymore—the owls of my youth say in my dad's voice, "Who hoots for you?" and the coyotes, while maybe on the hunt, calm me now and alleviate the weight on my chest.

❦

On one of the worst mornings I've ever had, I was driving, tears running down my face, hands shaking. As I drove, I prayed for strength for the day ahead, relief from the torture of my own mind. I almost drove past my destination, worrying if I could really deal with another day of obligations, unsure of how I'd make it. Caught in an ongoing cycle of worry, I cried and pulled my car over to the side of the road to compose myself. I cried more, mascara dripping on my cheeks, sobs kicking up my asthma and tightening my lungs. Unsure of how I could even continue driving, I simply sat. For me, when I feel this way, the best thing to do is to be still, silent. After a few moments, I looked up and there, on a rock in the river, was a bald eagle. It was sitting on the rock, sure and confident.

The river was beautiful, as it is on most days. The sun was shining, I remember, because I didn't understand how it could be so beautiful outside when inside all I felt was gloom and doom. I watched the sun dance on the white of the eagle's head before it took flight, soaring down the river. Like the day in the field, a partial relief flooded over me. I just stared at the river where the eagle had been, sure of only one thing: I could go on, if only minute by minute. Like in Isaiah 40:31, I gathered strength from my prayers and the image of the eagle sustained me.

On another day during those very hard months, I dropped the kids off at school and turned the corner to make my trek to work when I saw an acquaintance, a fellow mother. She and I had sat on a school committee together. I pulled my car over to say hello and she told me about her own early and similar morning practice of stillness: sitting with her cup of coffee in the wee hours of the morning, praying and meditating. Through the window of my car, she reminded me that my name had come to her mind one morning the week before and knew she had to tell me. She had emailed at the time, but she wanted me to know, in person, that my name was on her mind and in her prayers, and that small gesture was a sign to me that all would be well. Even if I wasn't sure how or why, I was reminded that the fog rises. Still, on other days, it's much less divine than that.

On days when the weight is almost too much to bear—the disappointments, and the guilt for seeing them instead of the blessings—I just go about my day, focusing on trivial matters of routine. Today, I got out the vacuum and pushed it along the edge where the floor meets the walls. The stink bugs are bad this time of year, our house being so close to the woods, and my hose catches the dead ones, the ones on their backs, tiny legs in the air. They don't smell anymore—their signature— and I wonder how long they've been there, there in the crack that's very hard to see, a gap where the molding simply leaves an opening, small but present. One by one, I vacuumed them up along with the dirt of the winter, focusing on the hose and the dirt, the sound of the floor being made clean again. I got snacks for children home from school, kissed their cheeks, always noticing, now that I've willed myself to, the color of eyes and hair, cheeks and lips, but today I noticed a small scratch on Matt's face. He told me the dog had scratched him while they were playing. My fingers traced the line that was in sharp contrast to the perfect complexion, save a mole or two, his olive undertones making the maroon of the scratch that much more vivid.

I unpacked lunch boxes; the pits in the uneaten

strawberries gave me pause—a bit of darkness in the splendor of red, the jubilance of strawberries that reminded me of how much my mom once loved her kitchen decorated with strawberries. I don't remember anything else about the kitchen, but I remember her face, alive with joy, when she talked about how much she loved it. I unloaded the dishwasher, glass by glass, and I reveled in how the light caught the etchings in them, the cuts so deep but so radiant. It was sunny and the sun revealed all error of dirt, every single dust bunny, but that glow was what called me to vacuum and clean up, the task helping me with the weight in my chest, the pain that literally feels real sometimes, that literally *is* real sometimes. These things are my life, and in them, the symbols aren't lost on me: the brokenness against the fixed, the dead among the living, the cuts in the otherwise flat glass, the scratch against the most perfect skin, the pits in the strawberry, so full of the juice of being alive. *They're like me*, I thought, and I kept vacuuming and unpacking, kissing foreheads and putting glasses away, and minute by minute, with the prayer of the routine, I emerged, the tightness fading, the pain easing, the beauty in the imperfect revealed. *Everywhere holy.*

Maggie, now four, rides her bike in the driveway, round and round, as I sit here at my desk and type. I can see her from my window, her hair bouncing as she rides her brother's old blue balance bike. She's always in my vision; that's the rule. And I can hear her singing, always singing. She's learning how to be alone, right outside my window and under my watchful eye, and she's changing. I can tell. Always a child who has delighted in the world at large and being around people, she now knows the peace it is to be alone, outside, on a gloomy and breezy day. These days are actually some of my favorites and despite the sun not shining, this daughter of mine seems to know well that the sun doesn't need to be shining in order to experience joy. Her joy is the bike on this dreary day and my joy is watching her ride it.

CHAPTER 2

Oh, the Rainbows in the Sky

My heart leaps up when I behold
A rainbow in the sky.
—WILLIAM WORDSWORTH

O ne Sunday morning at church last year, Matt leaned over and said to me, "Mom, look how the windows come alive with the sunlight as we sing. Every single time we sing, the windows light up." It was a sunny morning with only a few stray clouds and seemingly, as if on cue, the clouds retreated when we sang and the stained-glass windows came alive in all their varied colors, almost like a sign of a holy presence.

I believe we were given colors in the form of a rainbow as a symbol of God's promise to the earth and its people.[1] Forever, colors are to remind us of an everywhere holy. I've come to think of this as a way to live: to see the world alive with color—literal and metaphorical—and as a way to be thankful for all I have.

After the birth of both my children, I experienced motherhood like a storm that often comes before those rainbows we all love—the way the sky is so beautiful in an eerie way right before the clouds roll in over the green lush of the mountains. The sky, alive with colors of gray and pink—magical, really—was a harbinger of what was to come: a change was coming and it was unstoppable. I could feel the rain in my bones, the way I can now smell snow after a lifetime in Pennsylvania, but I had no idea what it would mean for me. I could see the colors in the sky, of course, but back then, I would seldom take the time to *see* them, appreciate them, understand them as the paint strokes of God.

Motherhood was as if a small child took all the pieces of me and threw them up into the air, and they were picked up by the storm. The storm turned into a tornado, and for quite some time, those pieces circled in a funnel. I felt disoriented and confused as all of whom I thought I was at thirty—carefully constructed and sure—metaphorically circled around me, pieces of my identity scattered here and there. When the tornado passed, as they always do (remember: *they always do*), I was left with the pieces of the Kara I had once been and had since become.

Over the years, I've picked up all of those pieces, but the puzzle of me is forever changed. It looks more like the little girl in the clearing used to. The colors in the world—similar to the colors in the sky before a storm—have come alive again for me, just as they were when I was a child, just as rainbows appear high in the sky after such storms, stories of color over mountains. Often, we're programmed to think of our days, of our *lives*, as something to "get through"—our lists and places we need to go and be—but we can change our perspective and realize the spiritual journey of seeing the world alive with color. That's not always easy, of course. Rarely is it.

Like other tornadoes that have come since then, the one I found in new motherhood was necessary for me, and it came to help me remember myself as I once was before the calculated exterior I had created in my twenties. Your metaphorical tornadoes may be different, but I'm sure they have been necessary for you. Like Dorothy in *The Wizard of Oz*, I became more appreciative of the life I had when the storm passed and I settled into the journey of motherhood. In life-changing moments like these, we grow and, in the end, we're never the same. That's been so very true for me. I've been taught how to live again—how to see beauty as I did before, to remember who I really am, and to find God everywhere.

Motherhood and the stage of middle life have been that way for me, but for others, it's not in the giving of life but in its loss that the lessons come.

∞

A few years ago, Mike's cousin, his childhood playmate, went missing. He had last been seen fishing on a bank by the Susquehanna River, a beautiful body of water, placid in some areas with white water in others, that cuts through Pennsylvania like a ragged-edged knife. The family was worried and filed a police report, but days passed with no sign of him. His brother, Mike's other cousin, assembled a small search party, and Mike was one in a group of men who set out in kayaks one hot Saturday morning in August to search for him.

Mike had struggled with faith for as long as I'd known him, but he said he felt pulled to go along. He wasn't sure how else to explain it, and when he looked at me, his blue eyes were filled with tears. I won't ever forget the look on his face—the conviction, the call he felt to go. In all the years I've known him—a lifetime, really—I'd never seen it before.

He drove two hours to meet his cousin at the riverside and after a short time at the riverbank, before they set forth on the river itself, they explored downriver. Mike told me he prayed as they walked and felt sure his cousin would be found that day.

And his cousin was found, facedown in the river; his

body was caught on a fallen sycamore tree—its colors of brilliant white and black, bark peeling—that kept him from floating downstream. He had been fishing and had fallen into the river. I've never seen my husband as broken and somber as he was when he told me this horrific news—crestfallen but so very sure of God, suddenly, only because of the call he felt to go and the ultimate discovery of his cousin. His cousin could now be taken home to his family to be laid to rest. And through it all, his death changed Mike.

I have been blessed never to have experienced loss or grief on the scale that causes these almost immediate sycamore tree transformations. My own journey has been more of a gradual realization, as the girl of my youth was squashed often by the pursuit of being something more, having something more, or doing more and more.

It wasn't until I became a mother that my world came alive again with beauty I hadn't noticed since my own childhood, there at my old house, there in the mountains. With motherhood came a changing of my life and the way I saw it. I was brought to my knees, literally, as I learned to mother my own children, and in return, they taught me how to find holiness and beauty everywhere again—how to cultivate it right there, right then, right *here*, right *now*.

The first time I held Matt, I was transformed. Like Dorothy in *The Wizard of Oz*, I found a yellow brick road, but for me, Matt was that road. He was my pathway back to myself as I once was. When he was laid on my chest, right after he was born, he lifted his heavy head up to look right at me. "Wow, he's a strong baby!" the doctor said, and it was the strength I saw in him that changed me. I saw God in his dark blue eyes, in his flawless face, his chubby hands. In that moment, I was a mother and I was changed, instantly, yes, but the journey had only just begun.

Of course, like other stages of life, these kinds of sycamore tree moments can be scary. Like Dorothy, I felt pretty lost, as I realized my life would never be the same again. It can't be. And that's just it: *the perception of my life changed.* I saw things I hadn't noticed since childhood; peonies smelled more beautiful than I had ever remembered. I made some decisions about my life—my career path and my workload—ones I never expected to make, ones I made in distress (when we're told never to make decisions!), but my own sycamore tree moment had begun, and the baby in my arms carried me as I carried him to a whole new world. As he grew, *I grew.* I mothered him, and I slowly remembered how to see everyday beauty again. I started to find the girl I left years ago at my old house. When Maggie joined us five years later, I was brought all the way to my knees through a struggle with postpartum depression, in another sycamore tree moment, another instant of seeing the colors all around.

Years later, when Matt was almost seven and Maggie was almost two, I opened the curtains in my bedroom and saw two fawn siblings at play in our front yard, in the flat part very close to our front porch. Every day in the summer, we see different fawns playing. They're born in the spring in the thicket to the left of our fruit trees and we often see them with their mother, eating apples or pears. Just this very morning, I saw them eating ripe cherries from our cherry tree.

But that morning, I saw something I had never seen before and called the kids to the window so they, too, could witness it. The deer were playing with a large ball my kids had left outside. We watched them play and were thrilled to witness such a perfect moment when one deer pushed the ball with its nose, only to run away with fright after. As these deer siblings played, I looked at my own children, in awe at the window, faces pressed to the glass, complete wonder and amazement on their faces as they watched the deer play where they did. It's a moment I'm not sure I ever would have noticed as keenly, but my son's red shirt matched the ball the deer played with. I saw how vibrant life really was that morning at the window and the fruit trees confirmed it even more.

We have many apple trees here at our house, and by mid-September they are heavy with the weight of the fruit. Day by day, and one by one, apples break away and drop to the ground where those deer pick them up. We often find half-eaten apples in our small orchard, discarded and left for our chickens to peck at when they are out of their coop and free-ranging. That same year, when Maggie was only two and it was our first fall at our current home in the country, she picked one of them up. She was so proud of her find and ran to me with it. That day, her little hands held the apple so perfectly, and as someone who always and purposely notices color as a way to stay grounded in the moment, grateful for the rainbows in my own life, I was struck by how the apple matched her outfit perfectly, coincidentally, as if it was meant for her hands. That day and on many days since, I spent time taking in my surroundings and realizing the simple blessing that really is. Even though my life is drastically different from Baby Suggs's in Toni Morrison's stunningly haunting and beautiful novel *Beloved*, I "pondered color" as she did at the end of her life.[2]

My daughter's eyes are the color of the ocean right before a storm rolls in—that slate blue with an iridescence from the sky as it turns eerie, just like that tornado sky. Her eyes were once the most royal blue I had ever seen and now, slowly, they are settling into the color of her daddy's, the boy I met when I was only six. For every year since then, I've stared at those eyes in his face and it's strange to see them slowly appearing in the small face of this little girl of ours.

The red of the apple she held was the kind of red that isn't even totally red yet; the apple was still partially yellow, speckled in the prettiest way. It wasn't strawberry red or cherry red but a subdued red that gives you the hope of what it could be if it were only tended to a bit longer. It was summer turning into fall, personified in an apple, as I walked through the trees with my daughter, a tended apple herself.

That day and on many days since, I spent time taking in all the color as I played with my daughter. We walked, her hand in mine in a rare moment. The one who usually runs and explores ahead of me, so independent in so many ways, she held my hand and walked. She kept looking up at me, amused by something our dilute calico cat, Lily, did or the way the red hawk called and circled. Back then, she thought everything was "so funny," and she threw her head back in laughter, her white teeth glistening, her curls glowing a honey color. By taking in the colors all around me, I can honor the life I've been given, and you can, too, even if there are times when this gift comes in ways not obvious and even if they don't *feel* holy at the time.

Ever since Maggie was little, before even turning one, she was obsessed with getting her nails painted and she very regularly threw fits to have the color she desired. I didn't have much variety in quick-dry nail polish, so one day, when she was still two, I suggested one of the only colors I had. When I opened the hot pink, she insisted I paint her nails a dark maroon that was almost black. After a while she finally agreed, only to push my hand away when I started to brush her nails. The bottle of polish flew out of my hand and paint splattered all over the bathroom, the rug, the cabinet, the tile, and on both of us. To this very day, nail polish speckles the grout of the tile floor. Out of frustration over the hot pink tile, I raised my voice, only for Maggie to wail, big, hot tears dripping down her face, red from a few seconds of crying. She has the kind of skin that blotches instantly, her emotions worn on her face for all to see. Her hair was so curly back then, and I watched as one lone curl bounced on her forehead to the rhythm of her sobs. I just stared at her for a second, then realized it was only nail polish after all.

I left the hot pink where it had fallen in an artistic pattern of lines and dots, and I scooped her up in my arms. I walked to the little sofa in my bedroom and held her, then cupped her hand with my own. As we sat there, the sun shone the most glorious light on her head, just like the rays in church through the stained-glass windows—almost as if to call my attention to it, saying, *A holy beauty is everywhere, Kara, especially right here.* I sat with her and said I was sorry. She squeezed my hand and said, "Mommy, I'm sorry too."

In that small moment, time stood still. I breathed in the smell of her hair and watched the sun play and dance on her curls. She was a rambunctious and busy toddler then and an active and talkative child now, and I wouldn't see life as I do now if it hadn't been for the push she gave me when she was born. I was reminded of the gift she is when the light flickered in her hair and she appeared to me like the lighthouse she's always been: the signal of the coast, the freedom from the drowning waves, the blazing light that has reminded me of my love of life, the fiery girl who will always light up a room. That day, she lit it up with nail polish and taught me a lesson at the same time: there is no mess too big to stop me from seeing life in color and to practice it on purpose.

అ

A few days ago, Frances, our goldendoodle, found a fuchsia-hued tennis ball behind the sofa. We have a chartreuse-green velvet sofa in the space between our kitchen and our living room. I was at one of my favorite antique stores when I stumbled upon the forty-dollar sofa. It immediately caught my eye because green is my most favorite color—all shades of it. When I sat in it, I knew it needed to come home with me, and now, it's where my dad takes a nap after Thanksgiving dinner and where backpacks collect at the end of the day. The ball was a treasure to Frannie, pride and joy really evident in her gait. I watched the ball in its startle of fuchsia against her white-cream fur, the chartreuse sofa, the fuchsia tennis ball, the white dog, all reminders to me of the comfort a life can be—a green sofa, a white dog, a fuchsia tennis ball—the comfort *the noticing* is for me, the comfort of seeing life in color.

When we notice moments like these, they end up defining us. Some are even the *camera lens coming into focus* kind of moments. I've had others, too, and after each experience, the world has seemed clearer, looked brighter and more colorful. What's your color moment? Seeing life alive with color is a spiritual practice. It means seeing the sun as it streams into the stained-glass windows as a rainbow of sorts and the bright hue of nail polish as a sacred reminder.

೧

Today, when the kids were at school, Frances and I took a walk. I like to walk and pray in the field across from our house, and since the hay was baled and the sun was shining, we set off on an adventure. The emerald-green grass reminds me of Ireland, a place I love so much and dream of often, the green carpet stretching across the hills, rolling into the almost navy mountains. Limitless. The sky was the prettiest cornflower blue with wispy clouds of white rolling, moving, as the earth turned. We crossed the small mountain stream that was running fast now from days of rain, and the dog's paws got muddy, a chocolate brown on her white-cream fur. She didn't mind and I didn't either when the water rushed over our toes and across my camo-colored sandals. Onward we went, wet paws and wet feet.

A pear tree was beginning to lose its fruit so I stooped and picked one from the ground and bit into its perfect yellow-green. We kept walking, stopping to take in the Canada thistle, pale purple against the green of the grass, the best contrast, the kind so effortless in nature. We spotted an orange sulphur butterfly and a pearl crescent one, fluttering across the sky, the yellow and orange of their wings avoiding Frannie's mouth as she leaped to swallow them. The grasshoppers jumped from my feet to hers, reminding me of the grass at my childhood home, so alive with grasshoppers, the ones that captivated my cousin on a visit when we were little girls, a thing she remembers still. They blended in but contrasted enough, olive green against the emerald. The goldenrod set off the entire scene, mustard flowers that make me sneeze but whose contrast makes the sky more beautiful. I told Frances to sit then, snapped a photo of her against the sky, her leash dangling from my arm, and sent the photo to Mike.

I turned and looked at the hill baled with hay, and I saw dragonflies—glittering, glimmering, dancing. Why were there so many? They danced through the field and we watched. They were electric blue and shimmery, fairy tale-like, and the clearing from my childhood flashed in my mind where I once saw a dragonfly and sat captivated by it. I knew I'd have to show my children later. After all, I've come to notice colors again because of them.

We turned and walked back to the house, a prayer on my lips as a redheaded woodpecker called me to notice him in the sky. Yes, there is beauty in this life, all alive with color, and in it, we can find the message: *holiness is everywhere*. Like Henry David Thoreau in *Walden*, we can notice that "Heaven is under our feet as well as over our heads."[3] Yes, yes, it is, in the rainbows above and the earth we walk on, grasshoppers in flight in the blades of grass.

CHAPTER 3

Spirit on the Move

All the while God was validating it with
gifts through the Holy Spirit, all sorts of
signs and miracles, as he saw fit.

—HEBREWS 2:4

M att said to me recently, as he recounted a story to me
for the second time, "Mom, can you please pay attention?" How many times do others tell us to pay attention?
It's something we've heard from our teachers, our employ-
ers, our parents, our friends, and even our own children.
I remember in high school and in college, during lectures,

I'd draw or write in the margins of my notebook, sometimes zoning out completely in my own imaginary world of images and poems. When I was a little girl, I would say to my mom, "Mom, are you *listening*?" Despite her efforts, she wasn't always. (Imagine!) Even now, there are days when my children are chattering on and I suddenly realize I can't remember a single thing they've said. I think many of us can say this about whole days too; sometimes we don't even remember what happened in the shuffle of life. But if we pay attention, we will notice signs of God at work right where we are. This also means listening to the earth as it speaks and to God as he works through it. We may find that coincidences are connected to bigger-picture messages and perhaps even lay out a path in front of us. The Spirit truly is *on the move*.

❦

The snowy December day I got a text from Maggie's preschool teacher saying Maggie was crying and struggling to walk, complaining of knee pain, led me down such a path. The teacher had to help her walk from art class back to the classroom and to the cafeteria for lunch. In a panic, my husband rushed to pick her up.

As soon as I saw her knee, I knew something was terribly wrong. Fine that very morning, her knobby knee was suddenly swollen to three times the size of the other. When we took her to the doctor, he sent us straight over to the pediatric floor at the hospital in the small city near our home.

By this time, it was getting late, the day ending in all its glory, but I could only think of Maggie's knee, and with each possible diagnosis, anxiety, more under control after months of struggle, crept back and a familiar weight started to settle. When the nurses tried to draw blood from Maggie, she screamed a pitch that shocked me and sent her worried older brother out into the hall to look at the Christmas tree decorated with blue lights and cupcake ornaments. Matt paced, but my attention was focused on the little girl whose face I held. Time after time, they pricked her but because she was so frantic, huge tears streaming down her red and splotchy face, her veins wouldn't cooperate. The doctor had ordered a large amount of blood from this tiny three-year-old, but the nurses were hopeful they had enough. We took a break as the blood was sent to the lab. We soothed the kids with root beer popsicles, and we all looked out the windows at the city, alive with the illuminations of Christmas. I'll never forget the twinkling lights that danced on my daughter's face and my son looking out the window, his arm around her shoulders.

When the nurses came back, they said they needed more blood. My heart fell and Maggie panicked. Tears filled my eyes, and my husband held her down, whispering in her ear to calm her as the nurses stuck her. Our son was in the hallway and his face showed fear, tears welling in his own eyes. I watched as the nurses held Maggie's body so my husband could cup her face in his hands. The vein wouldn't budge. She screamed and the only thing I could think of was this: *pray*. Out loud, but quietly, I started to say one of my favorite and trusted prayers, and as if on cue, the blood flowed, red, glorious, and victorious, from my daughter's arm to the needle. It was just like that. Matt was beside me by now and he looked at me with incredulous eyes that suddenly looked holy in the glare of the hospital room. I looked at him and said, "The prayer worked," and he hugged me. A nurse looked at us and smiled, tears in her own eyes. I think it felt like a holy moment to us all.

The nurse walked to the lobby only to return a few minutes later with a perfectly imperfect cross made of wood. She said she thought I would like it and she was right. I held it that night while we waited to hear about Maggie, who eventually recovered from Lyme disease, and now it's in a bowl by my bed with some of my other favorite things. It was a confirmation of holiness being everywhere that December night in the hospital room. Some might call it coincidence, but we knew that night it was much more than that: it was an everywhere holy moment, a reaching out that came back to us in the form of blood, a red-hot promise straight from the sacred heart that all would be well in the end.

‎ ‎

Many years ago, I worried about my first baby, Cedar, a golden retriever Mike got me for my twenty-first birthday. When we lived in Virginia Beach and Cedar was only a few years old, we left for a vacation in North Carolina. I can't remember the details of the vacation, but I can remember the

God breeze, as my sister, Kelly, calls it. We left Cedar with a good friend, a dog lover, someone we fully trusted with our only baby. Over the weekend, Cedar was on a boat with our friend's family and she jumped in the water, carelessly, her electric-green tennis ball in her mouth. She simply wanted to swim. There was nothing Cedar loved more than the water, the waves lapping against her, her golden retriever spirit making her thrive in the open water; swimming was her passion.

Once, months before, we threw the ball in the ocean over and over again, and Cedar never hesitated to run and get it. She never showed fatigue, but when Mike saw her struggling as her head buckled under the choppy waves, he dove into the water, swimming to her rescue. She would have drowned for love of that tennis ball and swimming. If you know any goldens, they're like that. From that moment on, we only threw the ball ten times and then made her stay on the shoreline, despite her constantly pushing her nose against the slimy, sand-covered ball in my hand. Over her fourteen-year life, that never changed, even though we did. Cedar was always constant.

The day she was on the water and swimming by my friend's boat, she somehow got separated from the boat and from my friend and her family. They frantically searched for her without telling me because my friend didn't want to upset me on what had been a last-minute escape from real life. While away in North Carolina, I received a phone call from my sister-in-law from Pennsylvania. Her own sister, also living in Pennsylvania, had gotten a phone call about a golden retriever someone had found. I was completely confused how Cedar could be in Pennsylvania, but then I remembered Cedar had two tags on her collar—one with our Virginia Beach number and one I had never taken off that had my old Pennsylvania number, left over from when I had lived in Pennsylvania while Mike, a submariner, was stationed in Virginia.

Because we weren't home and at our Virginia Beach number, the caller dialed the Pennsylvania number I had disconnected about a year before. Coincidentally, that old number was assigned to my sister-in-law's sister who knew we had a golden. She put the woman who had Cedar in touch with us and we got back to Virginia Beach and retrieved her.

All of it seemed like the work of some sort of behind-the-scenes heavenly phone line operator, holy angels flipping crystal-clear switches so the call got to a person who could help. If the telephone company back in 2001 had assigned my old number to any other person, we never would have known about Cedar and who knows if we'd have found her. She had swum to the shoreline, her ball still in her mouth, and ventured up onto someone's dock. When my husband arrived at the home, he found her happily resting in the spot of sun on the kitchen's terra-cotta tile, the ball by her nose, her deep golden color almost red in the light. It's a small thing, I guess, but in these instances of divinity entering our normal spaces, we are reminded of its presence through various messages. I've seen messages all around since that day years ago in Virginia.

By 2016, we lived in an old brick house in the middle of a small town in Pennsylvania. Even though we loved the house and the borough, we felt the urge to list the home. We didn't have our eye on another home, but the call to Mike was loud and clear. I tried to ignore it (and him!) until it was clear to me too. I had a nagging feeling, like someone was waiting for it, like someone had sent a wish for a house like ours. The nagging was persistent. While we'd always known maybe we would sell it one day and move to a more rural location, and in some ways, back to our childhood roots and my dream of the fields, mountains, and the clearing, we listed and sold the home quickly. It seemed someone maybe *was* waiting for it. While there were many things I was afraid I'd miss about that house—the emerald-green and canary-yellow stained-glass windows, the tiger-eye maple doors, or the walks with the kids to our favorite park or consignment shop—it might sound strange to say I was most worried about our lilac bush.

During our first year in the house, Mike and Matt bought me a lilac bush for Mother's Day and planted it by the garage. We had a tiny yard, but in the four years we lived and loved there, the lilacs thrived and the bush was full. Mike promised he'd plant me new lilacs once we figured out where we'd land, so I knew I'd have lilacs again, someday. We moved after the lilacs bloomed in one last generous, holy purple show, all shades of lavender and amethyst. Leaving that house was hard, but leaving the lilacs was the hardest for me. The memory of tiny, three-year-old hands helping big ones plant the bush for me in an unmistakable display of love.

We bought our new home—the one we live in now—in midsummer and the blooms of spring were far gone. When I walked through the house before we closed on it, I fell in love with the mountain views stretching out in front of the property. I did discover a small mountain stream and so much beautiful and lush green foliage, but I couldn't tell what kind of flowers we'd have. I searched for a lilac bush, but I didn't see one and I didn't say anything. After all, I knew that one way or another, I'd have lilacs again.

During our first spring, in a very overgrown flower bed to the left of our driveway, a lilac bush appeared through the brush, her blooms in brilliant purples, some so very deep they were almost maroon in color. I was elated at this single determined bush and happily cut a few blossoms for the counter. My lilacs had followed me to this place, the house on the hill, the place we'd bought in another complete act of trust.

Later that week, the kids and I were out exploring. We walked out the front door, down the wide brick steps, and to the left. We hadn't ventured too far yet because of all the brush and weeds—so much beauty, all overgrown. While we were out playing and exploring, we stumbled upon a big lilac bush, bigger than I'd ever seen. As it turns out, we have about twenty times as many lilacs at this home as we did at our previous home. Selling our home was hard on me and buying the house we're in—one with so many needed projects—was a blessing, but also not easy. Some of the best things never seem to be easy, do they? As the kids and I picked lilacs and we continued to play outside, I just smelled them, all the while thinking about the leap we took into the unknown and in pursuit of a dream and a return to the lives we loved so much as children. I was worried about the move but saw all the blessings that had come with it.

A year later, I was in the middle of a very full few weeks, and quite honestly, I'd been exhausted and battling anxiety and a three-day headache. I was out late, working, and when I came home, the house was dim and quiet; even my husband had fallen asleep. But there, on the counter, was a perfect vase of lilacs, cut and arranged for me by Matt. The smell of the lilacs hit me before I saw them, and the simple image of them reminded me that I was home with my people who know how much I adore lilacs.

To me, it's a powerful metaphor, a remarkable example in an ordinary object. It was a message to me, I think: *Yes, Kara, it's hard to change sometimes—leaving the metaphorical lilac houses.* It's hard to leave something we love and it's oh so, so hard to follow the call. The nudge comes and we ignore it for fear of what could be in the future. I've done it, time and time again. But that night, in the still hush of the house, the scent of flowers refreshed my spirits and I could not imagine missing out on this life on the hill with these lilacs. These everywhere holy reminders come on the regular now that I can see them.

Matt has a journal he loves, one with a fox on it. The fox is his favorite animal, a love he inherited from my father. My aunt Kate, my dad's sister, bought it for him because she instinctively knew he'd love it. She was right. Like my dad and me, Matt has a love of the red fox and writing; the journal is both. Matt writes poems and dreams, draws images, makes lists. One morning, when I was feeling particularly conflicted about my own path—teaching, writing, *all of it*—he showed me his list of dreams: to move to Boston, to go to Harvard, to become a doctor, to play for the Red Sox and the Steelers, and other things. They were all admirable things, all big dreams for a little guy. At the very end of the list, he wrote, "But above *all*, I want to serve God." I smiled at him and said how wonderful his dreams really are. He said, "Mom, do you know which one I can do right now?" I smiled, waiting for the answer I knew would come: "I can serve God." I just smiled softly at him, like I often do, rendered speechless for a few seconds, and I replied, "You know what, buddy? I can too." And it was like confirmation to me of a path, confirmation that while our dreams are big—mine, my son's, *yours*—we can serve as we seek and that *we can serve right where we are*. It was a renewal for me, one that came in an unexpected place, one I maybe once would have chalked up to coincidence. But once we open our eyes to the possibility of them, these renewals come, even amid our trials. I've learned the reminders are especially prevalent when we truly need them.

෧

I often stay awake at night, worrying. I've been doing this since childhood, and as a little girl, when I'd wake up on many nights, my own mom would be in her bathrobe in the orange chair in the living room in front of the stone fireplace, sipping tea, up from worry too. This habit has followed me into adulthood and has waxed and waned over the years. As I've learned to turn things over and sought help for anxiety, I've slept a bit better, but it's still something that happens on the regular, despite my best attempts and various strategies. It's partially just who I am now.

After being awake one night, worried about an issue with Matt at school, one that was causing Mike and me to question if he needed something different, maybe even a new school, I finally fell asleep. And in that rest, I had the strangest but most comforting dream.

Matt was on his way to Arimathea, and I was watching him walk away down a dirt road, dust encircling his head, tall mountains behind him, his summer shave making his head look almost white in the sun's summer rays. In the dream, I wasn't upset that he was walking away from me, which was surprising when I awoke because I never like to see Matt walking away. It's a bit of a struggle for me almost every time I drop him off at school. But in the dream, it was very apparent he was walking to Arimathea, and as he turned to wave and smile at me, I blew him a kiss. In the dream, I just knew he was setting off on a journey he was meant to take. I felt at peace about Matt and his path.

When I woke up, the place was fresh on my mind. The name, Arimathea, was not very familiar to me. I had heard the name but I couldn't remember the meaning or the significance and I had to research it. I've told you that I'm not at all a theologian, but apparently there's a lot of conjecture about the place—its meaning, its real location—but it shows up in the Bible as a city of Judea and the hometown of Joseph, a man who helped bury Jesus' body in his own tomb (Matthew 27:57–60). I'm not completely sure why I dreamed of this place, a world foreign to me, really, and I'm not exactly sure why my son was leaving for it in my dream. But I was comforted in the dream and comforted when I woke with peace about where Matt was and what he was doing. I suddenly was sure he was in the right place, just like Joseph was when he needed to be, and that all would be well, the kind of *all will be well* echo holiness delivers if we pay attention to the messages that show up in the unlikeliest places, even in the middle of dreams or even in bedrooms that need to be organized.

One weekend morning, after lots of coaxing (too much coaxing), Matt cleaned up his room. His room is often like a battle zone, LEGO bricks all over the floor. Have you ever stepped on a LEGO? I don't recommend it. Have you seen that meme of a shark in the ocean, leaping from the waves, its mouth open? Apparently, even a shark feels pain from a LEGO! I had stepped on one that morning and was frustrated about the state of his bedroom. I try to let my kids keep their rooms the way they see fit, but there are rules and I need to be able to walk in the room. Matt reluctantly cleaned up his room and I went to fold a never-ending pile of laundry in my own room as Maggie played. About ten minutes later, Matt called me into his room to inspect his progress.

His room was cleaned up and his bed was haphazardly made. LEGOs were put away, or rather shoved into his closet, and the closet door was closed. But my rule was followed: I could walk in there. I smiled and said, "Good work, buddy!" and was about to leave when he said, "Hey, Mom, look what I did." He pointed to his lamp; a clothespin he had found was holding up something, affixed to the shade of his lamp. I walked over and saw he had pinned the card my aunt Shari, my mom's sister, had sent to him. He had hung the necklace she had sent him on the lamp too.

When my uncle Scott died unexpectedly a few years ago, Matt wanted to get my aunt Shari a Saint Raphael necklace. It was his own idea and he insisted my husband drive forty minutes to get it. Matt had heard that he was an angel of healing and my aunt Shari was obviously mourning the death of her husband. He got her a necklace, and in the years since, they've shared a bond. She sent Matt a card and another necklace for him to wear, both hanging that morning on his lamp. He told me it reminded him of her and my uncle and that made him happy. I took a quick photo and sent it to her.

Minutes later, I got a text back from her telling me she had been at my uncle's grave that very morning when Matt was cleaning his room. She had asked my uncle for a sign that he was watching over the family. Only an hour later, I took the photo and sent it to her. To her, it was a godsend, a message, a sign asked for, a confirmation that my uncle was still a part of her life even if he wasn't physically present. This has shown up in other ways too—messages from those who are only with us in spirit.

Early one cold November morning in 2000, I got the call that my sister, Kelly, had gone into labor. It was her first baby, the child who made me an aunt, and the first grandchild for my parents. To say we were all excited is a total understatement. But the baby was five weeks early—far enough out from his due date that we all were a bit nervous as she headed to the hospital with her husband. Kelly ended up having a healthy baby boy before I even got to the hospital. My parents were already there, proud and relieved the baby and my sister were safe. I didn't realize, though, that my nephew was born on my grandfather's birthday, my father's father. He was known as Buddha, an old nickname from his military days. He died when my father was in his early twenties and my siblings were small. I never had the privilege to meet him, but Kelly sure did and called him Pop-Pop Buddha. My dad had been close to him and Buddha had gifted my father with a love of the outdoors and nature and, as it seemed that November day, the gift of my sister's first child and my father's first grandchild. I like to think of Pop-Pop Buddha handing Kelly my nephew, that God allowed him that privilege. I picture him kissing my nephew's nose before he handed him over. My father and nephew have always shared a special bond, and my father has passed the love of nature and the outdoors on to him, straight from Buddha.

It's easy to chalk all these stories up to coincidence. When three doves visited my sister's yard on a Fourth of July after my brother-in-law set off the fireworks and they were over, the doves stayed for just a moment, enough time for us all to notice them before they flew away. My mom and I both stopped and stared, both of us pretty sure it was a sign, and even if it wasn't, the beauty was in the noticing. Most people might just think it was a coincidence and not a harbinger of peace and love. But, deep down, I've always known there was something more to these things, even if it feels safer to have explanations. I'm sure you have stories just like it—uncanny coincidences you can't explain. What messages are trying to reach you? How can you open your eyes to symbols or coincidences in your own life? If you can start noticing, I think you'll be so surprised at all the holy intercessions, right in your own life, right where you are, helping you understand that holiness is all around.

CHAPTER 4

Right Here, Right Where I'm to Be

God himself culminates in the present moment.
—HENRY DAVID THOREAU, *WALDEN*

When I was a little girl, one of my favorite songs was "The 59th Street Bridge Song (Feelin' Groovy)" by Simon & Garfunkel. As a child I loved the images in the song and always imagined I was *in* the song—dancing along to the tune and taking the time to stop to look at the life all around me, right where I was. When I heard the song, I pictured I was on Sesame Street, smiley and happy, stopping to chat with Big Bird or Grover (my favorite) or trying to make Oscar the Grouch smile. Back then, like most children, I knew how to live in the moment, and the song has always reminded me of the simple glory that is.

If you look around at the children in your own life, you can see most of them know how to live in the moment; however, most adults I know have lost that ability, at least from time to time. Which has left me with this question: How can we see the gift our lives are if we can't learn to stand in the here and now, appreciating the gifts of the second, hour, day instead of projecting, planning, and just waiting for the next best thing? It's hard, I know. But we have to try. By trying to see the present day as the holiest of gifts, we can then appreciate the life we have simply by living it. By learning that there's no rush to an imaginary finish line and by learning to slow down, I think we really can see holiness everywhere and welcome it into our lives, on its own terms, as it comes in the smallest of ways. Often, for me, that comes in the form of the most menial and daily tasks.

In the silence of the house, I was overwhelmed with the list of tasks in front of me. The sun trickled through the window above the white farmhouse sink I love, an old trivet that once belonged to my parents behind the spigot. I grew up with the trivet, a pastoral scene—a man tending animals, children, a stream, mountains. My mom had put it in the yard-sale bin one summer and I gasped, grabbing it and peeling off the one-dollar sticker she had on it. She chuckled, not knowing

I had loved it so much, and said, "Take it." Like all things I have here at this house from my childhood home, the trivet takes a prominent place for me, coincidentally, the reminder to me of the people and things I love most—a man, children, animals, water, mountains. I sat and stared at the trivet for a minute, having just put on the water for my morning tea.

To the left of the trivet, the sun shone on the previous day's eggs from our hens, still waiting to be cleaned, dried, and put into the refrigerator. I decided to start my task list there, with those thirteen eggs, and one by one, I washed and rinsed them under the stream of water, carefully handling them and scraping dirt, chicken poop, and feathers from the shells. One by one, I studied them, their varied colors and markings taking me away from the stress of my list— the one I made a few days prior and lost just as quickly as I made it. Pushing back feelings of failure for losing my list and for a million other things I've failed to do in this lifetime—the weight of that sometimes so heavy I struggle to breathe under it; the weight feels that real sometimes, that tactile, that much of a real-life stone—I washed the eggs, carefully taking in the details of them the way a mother studies her children's hands and feet fresh from the womb, counting fingers and toes. One by one, I turned them, lost in the eggs themselves, the speckles and lines, the varied shades of brown, cream, and peach. Some were perfectly patterned, some irregular, some small, and some quite large. Each egg had my attention, and even as I heard Frances chewing my husband's shoe, nothing could distract me from my task at hand. Turning each egg and putting it on the cloth to dry a bit in the sun, I washed all thirteen and then took a towel and dried each of them, placing them in the egg carton.

The teakettle roared, and Frances pounced, tossing the gray shoe higher and higher in her own game, the house alive, suddenly, the sun calling us, the light of it so bright that if you saw it that morning you wouldn't have been able to stop looking toward it. The list awaited, the day beginning, but my time with the eggs was sacred time, observation as prayer, routine as an offering. I put the eggs in the fridge, walked over to the dog and took the shoe, and turned off the roaring kettle, the steam billowing from its pale-green spout. I poured my tea into my favorite mug, a smooth one with a watercolor of a rooster that looks like Henry, my rooster, and I sat by the window, for just a minute, and the day began. I made another list, but the few minutes spent washing eggs ended up granting the peace I needed, all because I stopped to notice the beauty of the eggs in the same way I often watch the beauty of the sunrise over the mountain.

Last spring the weather in Pennsylvania could best be described as an insolent child throwing a tantrum, the way Maggie sometimes did a few years ago while we were out shopping. Her tantrums were splendid, in the very worst ways, just like the weather that spring, so very outrageous as to be admirable. The weather was finally pacified after days and days of rain, hail, snow, and cold temperatures, all in April. The toddler named Weather finally seemed happy, and I watched the sun come up over the mountain while

Maggie slept beside me. She's always in our bed by the morning, her face buried in my pillow, the covers only revealing her mop of curls. I watched the sun rise over her head, the light always amazing me, always coming after the darkness of night, casting her in a holy glow like a halo. Holy sun, holy hair, holy child.

The weather seemed joyful and when I walked toward the school where I teach, the smell of the fresh bark mulch reminded me, *Yes, it is spring. Yes!* the birds called and the dove cooed. I stopped and looked for the dove, but I couldn't find it in the recesses of the buildings or in the trees that shade the back of the campus. My boots hit the pavement, my line straight ahead and right along the edge of the sidewalk, the rhythm keeping beat with my prayers, the prayers I always say as I walk from my car, down the steps, across the walkway, and down two more flights of steps, before walking up the building's stairs to my second-floor classroom, ending with a simple prayer, right before I open my door: *God, please remind me I'm right where you want me to be.*

I opened the door of room 208 into the heat of my classroom, the thermostat turned up from days of cold that had passed but the switch now forgotten. The bell rang as I slipped in the door to its sound. The sun I watched rise that morning was shining through my classroom windows, a view I've cherished for years—nature being visible has gotten more important to me again and I could see it there in the school on the hill, all varied shades of green, all alive and beautiful that morning. While there was the bustle of a day beginning and activities and grades to turn in, the quiet word I heard—only in my own ears—was *here*. And so I hung my bag on the coat hook I keep by my desk, got out my water bottle, took a quick drink, and turned to my class; the faces of my students waited for me. The teaching day began right in that quiet *here*. I've heard that word in other ways too.

One winter morning, I drove down a side street where construction on the sidewalk was occurring. I was annoyed about the construction and the coffee I had spilled on my white shirt as a result of the uneven pavement. I love wearing white T-shirts (I have about ten of the same one!) though I'm not sure why; inevitably, they end up with coffee on them. I was driving slowly, of course, and decided to take the time to admire the old houses on one of the prettiest streets in our town. As I glanced over, I saw a mother and baby in a big, arch-lined window, tiny arches of cut class at the top, like a church window. The mother was looking at the child with pure adoration as the child looked at the construction equipment and giggled. I caught a simple and beautiful moment—just a second of a life they lead, but it told me so much. As I drove through the construction, I fondly remembered the days when my own task was bouncing a baby and watching life unfold beyond the windows. That stage was a beautiful one but so is this one. When we look at moments like these, we really can see holiness everywhere, and sometimes, that's the view from a car window or even in discarded shoes in the yard. It's the paying attention that helps reveal the holy beauty all around.

Another morning, I did my very best to stop and notice the monarch butterfly that alighted on my daughter's shoe left discarded in the yard so she could run barefoot: her favorite, like I used to. My first thought was this: *How many times do I ask my children to bring their shoes in from the yard?* But if it hadn't been there, I wouldn't have noticed the contrast of the butterfly's brown and orange wings against her pink shoe with the rainbow soles, still shimmering from the morning dew. A rainbow, right there in the yard, calling me to see color, God's promises. The butterfly stayed there long enough for me to notice and to realize the beauty of it all. It was spectacular, really, a small (but big?) reminder that this life really is holy enough, standing right here, right now, right where I was, and I know it now, as Mike reminded me.

He and I were reminiscing about our 1995 prom recently. We both went with different people to the prom, but we ended up leaving the after-prom together (scandalous, I know!). We'd been friends since childhood and our relationship took a turn that April night and over the summer that followed. That summer turned and spun into forever, really, rolling into this life we have now, like the mountain hills roll here in central Pennsylvania. I remember it like it was yesterday, and he does, too, and I said to him, "I'd love to go back there to the summer of 1995, just for one day." We were young, in love, and that summer seemed carefree. We'd go to our jobs and hang out after work, hiking, sitting by the water of the lake, listening to music. My favorite CD back then was Tom Petty's *Wildflowers*, and I really did feel like my place was in a field, like the field of flowers I treasured by the road at my old house, all black-eyed Susans, goldenrod, and magenta-purple phlox. I think I knew then what I wanted my life to look like, but somewhere along the way I forgot and spent the next twenty-three years trying to remember. Life wasn't always easy for me then, but during the summer of 1995, I was falling in love and it turned out to be one of the best summers of my life. It wouldn't be until the summers my babies were born that anything came close to that one when I was sixteen.

I said all this to him, and I said how I wished I had known then what I know now. He smiled softly at me, squeezed my hand, then looked at our kids, and said, "Someday, we're going to say the same thing about right now. Except we know how good we have it." He's right. Learning *here*—I mean, learning to *be here*, right now, right here—isn't always easy, but it is worth the effort. We will sometimes lose our way in this pursuit of learning here, but trust me: when we can stay in the moment, the rewards are great. That was particularly clear to me one morning; the rewards of learning to be here in the now came to me in shades of purple.

I was up early and watched the sunrise one morning during Lent, the sky slowly coming alive in its shades of purple. Slowly announcing the day, the sun murmured, "I'm on my way." She took her time, for she knows well how it takes us all time to adjust to so much light after the darkness of night. The purples extended over the mountains, almost like an invitation; the lilac of her hand beckoned me to a new day.

The purples are my favorite, especially that first Sunday of Lent, the first weekend of the wait. The sun was a message from the Caller. And we are the called. I sat and watched and prayed in the silence of the morning, before the house came alive with its own sounds of early morning, its own shouts of children and barks of the dog. Soon, I knew I'd hear Henry, our rooster, his crow replacing the hoot of the familiar owl. Soon, the day would begin with the hustle of a full calendar. But then, I sat, as one who was called—the called to the here and now.

This here-and-now approach is a simple beginning, a more generous invitation to see the holy beauty everywhere. Once, when we were on a trip to the beach with my parents, my kids kept asking, "Where are we?" and "Are we there yet?" My father said, "We are right where we are to be. Where else would we be?" He's right. By remembering that we're right where we're to be, maybe we can finally under-stand that life isn't meant to be rushed through. Maybe we can *finally* stop overextending ourselves in order to prove ourselves worthy because the most important thing is to appreciate the *now*. I did that for too long—that chaotic shuffle for approval, the forgetting to be right where I am—and I grew tired of it. I suspect *you're* tired of it. Now, being right where I'm to be, means that listening to our ducks quack and watching the deer and children play are often my prayers: these are small but essential steps. Sure, I might have shoes discarded in my yard and too many papers piled on the counter. My list might be long, just like yours. Yes, I still might overextend myself, saying yes instead of no, like I'm sure you sometimes do, but I'm learning to take the time to look at what this life really is. It begins with noticing the seemingly ordinary moments of life, the washing of the eggs or even staring out a window at construction equipment. Seeing them as a way to see God everywhere is a way to welcome holiness and to see the life you've been given as *good enough*. Holiness is all around, in the end, but we need to start by seeing it in our own places, right where we're to be.

Tonight there were toys all over the yard and tools left over from a landscaping project. I knew I should pick them up or someone should, but before I did or hassled someone else to, I spent a few minutes taking in the view. Maggie fed our chickens red-ripe strawberries from her hand and then played in the garden. She was still in her floral school dress, reminding me of the girl I once was, playing in the yard in an old-fashioned dress with an eyelet overlay I had been given as a hand-me-down that always reminded me of *Anne of Green Gables*. Matt's hair was thick and unruly, like my brother's always was when we were kids. He kicked the soccer ball in the yard and Frances ran for it, time after time, bringing it back to him. Mike mowed the lawn with his riding mower and I remembered how my dad loved his old red tractor and mowed similar lawns with it. I simply leaned on the side of the brick steps, watching my people as they reminded me of a similar scene from long ago. What a gift. The sun sank low over the ridge and I just watched it all unfold, right there, right where I was to be, the present God all around.

CHAPTER 5

They, So Fresh from God

I love these little people; and it is not a slight thing
when they, who are so fresh from God, love us.

—CHARLES DICKENS, *THE*
OLD CURIOSITY SHOP

When I studied abroad in England, I took a class where we studied the work of Charles Dickens, and a line of his resonated with me even then, well before I had children of my own. He once wrote, "I love these little people; and it is not a slight thing when they, who are so fresh from God, love us."[1] I have always loved that line, and I remember holding my newborns and thinking of God kissing their little noses before sending them to me to hold, whispering in their ears their purposes, ones maybe later they'll spend years trying to remember, like I have. The image of them being held in God's large and ever-stretching hand was calming, and even now, when I look at my children, I think of that visual. Our children are held by God and we are, too, because we are *his* children. Through the children around us, I think, is one way to remember our own dreams and our own identities. I've been so astonished at the profound and simple ways my own children have *led me back* to who I was, to the girl at the house in the mountains.

Of course, you don't need to have children of your own in order to know what childlike wonder is or to be led back to it all. If you've ever spent time with the children of friends or family members, then you know what I mean. As we pay attention to the things they love, we just might be reminded of things we've forgotten we love too.

In my own English classroom, I always ask my seniors a question when we get to our unit on identity, when we read Franz Kafka's *The Metamorphosis*, Shakespeare's *Hamlet*, and various amazing poems by Mary Oliver, Adrienne Rich, Jamaica Kincaid, and Elizabeth Bishop. I'll ask you the same question here: *Who were you at the age of five?* Maybe now you're making the same face they usually do. They stare at me like I'm crazy and then all proclaim, "I don't remember!" I laugh and say they must try to remember. Then I give them questions to help them remember: Who did you play with?

Where did you love to spend time? What was your favorite toy? What kinds of things did you like to do or see? Slowly, they recall memories. Slowly, we all *must* remember because in doing so, we perhaps can remember our purpose, whispered in our ears before birth. I believe many of us have simply forgotten.

When I was five years old, I was a country girl who lived a simple life. I loved playing outside, and while I did have one very good friend—the neighbor across the dirt road we lived on—I played alone as often as I played with her. I was the youngest in a family of three children; my brother, Ray, is five years older than me, and my sister, Kelly, is almost eight years older than me. While they'd play with me sometimes, humoring me—Kelly setting up tea parties or Ray building an igloo out of snow one winter for us to play in—I played alone a lot. As the baby of the family, I always, always wanted to be older, and I spent much time observing them and the other adults around me.

Years before, when I wasn't quite three, my parents moved to the country from a working-class suburb of Philadelphia. Unlike my sister, who was older when we moved and missed riding her roller skates and bike on the sidewalks, I loved the feel of dirt and grass on my bare feet and the filtered light in the woods behind our house. As I grew, I spent a lot of time reading about magical, imaginary worlds and often talked to myself, the many animals at our house or at the farms around us, and to God, as if he were a friend. My most favorite thing to do was to read, but I also

loved music. My parents often played records in the house—
Bob Dylan, Crosby, Stills, Nash & Young, the Beatles, the
Rolling Stones. I started playing the piano around the age of
five and took lessons at a farmhouse down the road. Music
was another way for me to visit places in my imagination,
getting lost in the stories I heard in the songs. I loved to draw
and spent time sketching butterflies, birds, and flowers—all-
natural things. While all those things were true for me then,
they're also true for me now, but I had forgotten, temporarily, until my children reminded me of the loves I had then.

Who were you when you were five? What things did
you like? Jot them down and dwell on the memories. Then
maybe you will remember pieces of your identity, perhaps
lost for a long time. And as you remember and gather pieces
of your own puzzle, perhaps you can slowly reassemble, as
I'm doing.

For me, it took becoming a mother—and other sycamore tree moments—to find myself again. I needed that
unraveling, the coming undone, really, for my identity to be
remembered and reassembled. Not everyone does, but I sure
did. I needed to fall apart so I could pick up and begin anew.
Over and over again, my children have reminded me of the
little girl I once was, of the heart I had for creative work,
and the joy I found in the little things. I truly believe children
will lead us if we let them, and if we don't have children of
our own, we learn from the ones around us. When we follow
them, maybe we can remember who it was God truly put us
here to be and that we, ourselves, are God's children.

❧

As a little girl, one of my favorite activities was walking to the end of the dirt road I grew up on to watch the cows at the farm on the corner. They were always in the pasture by the barn. I'd stand on the bottom fence post yelling "Moo!" until a brown cow sauntered over. My feet rested perfectly on the rung and I didn't care much about the flies circling around the pasture beyond the barn. But I had forgotten this, mostly, until we moved to our current home. Shortly after we moved here, my family and I were out for a walk and discovered a pasture of cows at the farm a field over from our house.

My daughter, not quite three at the time, was so excited and I honestly was too. She yelled, "Cows!" and we ran to watch them. I was completely in awe of them, as she was. I couldn't remember the last time I had simply stood and watched cows in a pasture. How long had it been? Decades? We stood and watched and she giggled. My husband walked up to me and said, "This is why we moved here. This right here." And as I stood there, holding the hand of my daughter while my son and husband walked on, a gust of wind was a confirmation: *Yes, Kara. This is it.* Our hair blew in the breeze—a God breeze, maybe, in my hair, dark next to her blond head. It was a true moment of feeling holy all around, a true moment of allowing a child to lead me back to where I began, the me *still there*, after all. That sunny spring day being led back looked like cow watching. It reminded me of my love of animals, nature, and of the still I can only find outside. On other days, it's looked like other things, even discarded cardboard boxes.

When we moved to our current home, we stored many, many boxes in the basement—things we didn't need right away, things we wanted to sort through, things we ended up forgetting about. Recently, one side of the basement took on a bit of water after a heavy rain. In an effort to clean up the water and sort through the damages, Mike and Matt moved boxes and boxes. Maggie and I were out at the time, and we arrived home to the familiar smell of Pine-Sol, something I never use but my mom always did, and Matt's excited smile.

"Mom," he said. "I found some of your old things!"

I smiled back as he took my hand and led me down to the basement. Literally, a child led me back—back to boxes of things I had forgotten about. Back to myself, really, as I left her packed up years ago. He showed me an old jewelry box with gold cross-shaped earrings and silver dragonfly earrings, both gifts from my mom. He showed me a photo album of my childhood my dad had compiled for me and given to me the night before I was married. He showed me a book I'd written and illustrated: a small watercolor-filled book I made for Mike for our first wedding anniversary. He showed me boxes of books and letters—one from one of my dearest high school friends to my husband when he was in the navy and so, so many letters between Mike and me when the only way we could communicate was through them. He showed me an old doll I loved, Madeline, and another doll I had gotten on a school trip in third grade when my mom was a chaperone and I slept in her lap on the way home from Bedford Village, the doll curled in my hand. I was never too big to rest my head in my mom's lap. As I stood with the items in my hands, I looked down and almost cried. I was reminded of all I once was (and maybe still am?). Matt was reminding me of all the good and the holy, right in the middle of the basement smelling like Pine-Sol, in the remnants of a life gone by.

It could be considered ironic or even coincidental that he did this when I returned home that night. I might have thought that myself before I learned what seeing holiness everywhere really *looks* like in real life. But now I know it can talk to us right in the dirty basement, right in the mess of the water, with our boots on and our jeans rolled up. Right from the hands of a child who sees your life, suddenly, as it was and you as you were, yes, but the you he can see *through it all*, even now. Children see through all of it to the *real* you.

That very day, I had come to a conclusion before I returned home: I needed to go back to who I was, more and more. And the letter from one of my childhood best friends to my husband? That friend had texted me just a few days before telling me an R.E.M. song had reminded her of me. I had forgotten, but then *I remembered. I love R.E.M.!* The book he found? It was on the same day I found out from my agent that this very book you're reading, the one I almost never sent out, had made it to the final round at a few publishers. None of these things were coincidences; I know they were messages.

If there is a box in your basement or attic with some of your childhood relics, put down this book and go get it! What stories do the objects tell? Why did you keep them at all? What parts of you have been packed up in the box, just waiting to be uncovered? What messages are there for you? Once we pay attention, these messages are all around, often right in the faces of our loved ones, which leads me to my next question: What is your very first memory? Dig deep, okay? Spend some time thinking on this one.

෨

My Pop-Pop, my mom's father, was only forty-nine years old when he tragically passed away from a heart attack, and he holds my first memory. I was just a little girl who adored him, just like my own little girl adores my father, whom she calls Pap. Everyone tells me how attached I was to him. I was the little one who lived around the corner in suburban Philadelphia before we moved to the mountains four hours away. I'd crouch down behind the orange chair my parents bought in the late seventies, right before I was born, and wait for him to come see me after he was finished working. Or I'd wait with Meemom at their house, by the window with Brandy, his Saint Bernard I loved.

It might sound odd, but my first memory is of Pop-Pop's blue eyes. He used to bounce me on his knee and I'd look in his eyes and giggle. I don't remember much about him or the time in the suburbs, but I remember very well how he made me feel. He had the bluest eyes, and I guess that's why I remember them. I heard somewhere once that children are often attracted to shiny or iridescent objects. I'm not sure if that's true, but his eyes glistened in the memory I have of him, of staring into his face, giggling and bouncing on his knee. For years I've analyzed this very brief memory, but I know the memory is real and it's mine. It *is* mine and his eyes were shining like crystal-blue diamonds.

I know it was his eyes that began my love of blue eyes in general. I feel his eyes on me now, all these years later, as I mother my children, one of whom has similar eyes. Maggie's eyes might not be his but her daddy's, though I secretly like to think that out of all of us, my sweet girl, who loves her own Pop the way I loved my Pop-Pop, has his eyes for me to look into, the light making them shine like blue diamonds too. *That's a gift from the other side* is what I thought when she was born and her eyes were so blue. I think that still. I think both of my kids are gifts from the other side—gifts Pop-Pop and others have helped to orchestrate.

Most mornings, I wake to those blue eyes (*Maggie's? Mike's? Pop-Pop's?*) and I have learned to embrace them, even though there are times in the night I wish she had stayed in her own bed. But I know well how I will miss waking to her blue eyes staring at my face, rubbing it as if it's the most important thing to her. On a recent morning, her first words were, "Mommy, I saved you." Not sure if I had heard her correctly, I said, "What?" and she repeated, "Mommy, I saved you."

Of course, she was fresh from sleep and perhaps at the very edge of a dream about a monster or a witch or something, but her words were so very true and I told her so. Her words stayed with me all day and I wondered how she knew which words to say. I have never once told her she saved me, although I have thought it. She did save me, my girl with the blue eyes like my Pop-Pop's. My daughter is the sun for me, and in the end, both of my kids saved me from the disaster of who I thought I wanted to be: *the me who wasn't me at all.*

First my son, who was like water to parched soil, forging paths in the mountain that was me, the way only water can. He's water to me—soothing but forging, changing me with the water of his birth and his life. Then Maggie—the sun, the fire—followed and warmed us all, the way only sun and fire can. And both of them—water and the fiery sun—made me grow; they make me grow every day.

I once thought parenting was about the parent teaching the children, or saving them even, when they needed it. And, of course, it is. But what I didn't know then that I know well now is they do the same. They teach me and save me just as much as I do them. Water and sun. Nothing grows without them. Both save life, and they saved mine. They've grown me. In the end, the growth—the saving—it's mutual. And how holy is that? How have the children in your own life changed you?

Once, we were outside enjoying the first day of spring snow, that anomaly that is Pennsylvania, the dichotomy of spring and winter—one so hesitant to let go, to let the growth and green and life come. My son and I were building a snow fort, or he was and I was watching him. Then we piled up snow-balls in the perfect fort, nestled under a tree for our snow battle with Mike and Maggie. We were making snowballs and I was thinking of the fire inside the house and a hot cup of tea, a distraction from the cold of my hands under my gloves, the Raynaud's disease making my one finger feel numb. My son noticed two woodpeckers and he excitedly told me to look up. From where I was, I couldn't see them at all and said so to him. By this time, he was lying in the snow and said to me, "Mom, see them from my perspective. Lie down. Look up from here." His words hung in the air, filled with meaning, loaded and so obvious—*see them from my perspective.* Could it be that simple for us? Simply a switch in perspective?

I lay down. I looked up. I saw the woodpeckers with their red heads and black-and-white spotted wings—two of them—pecking in the tree above us, the contrast of the red and the white never lost on me. From his perspective, the world looked so different, and if I hadn't stopped and lay down, I wouldn't have ever seen the world, in that time and space, as he did. He and I lay there, watching the wood-peckers at play in the trees, pecking away—friends, maybe? I reached my gloved hand for his and he squeezed my hand.

Months later, I went to church alone one morning, as I sometimes do. We'd all been up late and the kids were tired, snotty nosed, and with the cold rain of the morning, it just seemed easier for me to venture out by myself. Easier isn't always better, but after weighing the options and the reality of how things might go down in church and the germs the kids could spread, I pulled my hair up in a bun, threw on my rain boots and raincoat, and left everyone else on the couch with blankets, the snuggles on that Sunday prayers of their own, holy enough that morning.

When I walked into church, I went into the last pew on the right, slipping in right before the processional. I noticed two small children in the pew with their mother and grandmother but directed my attention forward. Many things weighed on my mind, and as I held my head in my hands, I prayed for wisdom in many areas. Often, church is therapy for me. That might seem selfish to some for me to say that—that I go often to take instead of give—but it's very true for me and for many of you, maybe, and in the end, I know God knows it anyway. Like some of you, I go to feel whole again, to center in on real issues, and to seek guidance.

As I glanced to my right again, I saw the two small children silently playing. The little boy had lined up army figures—the kind of army men many of us had or our brothers had, the kind that come in a bag of fifty for about one dollar. He had them all lined up, facing the back of the church. I caught his eye and smiled and he smiled, too, and then turned back to the play in front of him. The figures were bright red and green, lined up ceremoniously in a perfect and straight line, and were diligently fighting whatever creature the boy had imagined standing in the back of the church by the door.

About ten minutes into the service, a couple arrived with a toddler and a baby seat covered with a blanket. They sat in a pew across from me, a few rows up. When they got settled, they took the baby from his car seat. He was tiny, maybe just a few weeks old. The mother sat and cradled him in her arms, the length of him fitting just beyond her elbows. Palms up, she cradled his head in both of her hands, his body running the length of her forearms. His eyes were closed and a perfect light from the hanging pendant shone from above, right onto his tiny features. He was breathtaking, really, the way newborns are, and I stared at him for a minute. Just as I was about to look away, he made one of those sleepy, dreamy smiles that babies smile, as if they remember something none of us do, that sure smile of total and complete peace and comfort maybe only babies feel. His smile caught the attention of an older couple in the same pew and of a friend of mine sitting a few pews ahead of me. Despite the fact that we all were in a church, listening to a traditional service, I think we'd all say that watching that sweet baby was the holiest of all.

As I watched those children sleep and play, I was left with this: children will lead us. In our times of worry and doubt, they'll line up soldiers, so sure of triumph, and remind us that, truly, there's nothing too big for God and his workers, his angels, his hierarchy of all things seen and unseen, his own soldiers. Children, with their peaceful smiles, heads up in their mothers' outstretched palms, metaphors in their own ways, can truly help us find beauty everywhere by watching what they still remember. I challenge you to watch the children you spend your life with. Watch how they approach life. Follow their lead. It's pure magic.

A few days later, on a walk up the mountain behind our house, Maggie walked ahead of me, sure and always the leader, no matter where she is. She insisted on leading, as usual, and Matt relented, choosing instead to abandon our nature walk and run in the field with the dog. Mary, our cat, followed us on our walk as she usually does, staying behind Maggie but never too far behind. She followed, a watcher at her back, the small girl ahead of her the one she always keeps an eye on. Smaller than Maggie, the cat seems ever sure of her own might, just like the girl, my daughter, small but mighty. Both were so sure of each step, one white paw mirroring one pink Converse, step by step up the mountain.

I walked slowly, taking them in, breathing in the cool, end-of-day air and their spirits, their sureness, their unwavering confidence as they treaded up, up, up. I'm continually amazed at how they walk, but it's what helps me remember how I once was. It was just us—Maggie the leader, Mary and me the followers. Maggie was in the light, the sun calling my attention to her, and I noticed. My shadow loomed, but she was free from it; her body was completely in the rays of the early evening, the mountains already turning the most brilliant shades of navy and periwinkle. She said, "Mama, let's go." I followed, up the mountain, behind the girl who knows the way.

CHAPTER 6

Snow on Daffodils

"I wonder if the snow loves the trees and
fields, that it kisses them so gently? And then
it covers them up snug, you know, with a
white quilt; and perhaps it says, 'Go to sleep,
darlings, till the summer comes again.'"
—LEWIS CARROLL, THROUGH
THE LOOKING GLASS

Years ago, when Maggie was two, she pointed to a snow-
covered daffodil making its way from the earth and
asked me what it was. I answered, "That's the dream of

spring trying to make her way to us." It seems spring is sometimes delayed here in Pennsylvania. Just this past April, it snowed again, falling on the brilliance of the daffodils that had finally started to bloom—their yellow so alive, they seemed ready to dance, like they do in a Wordsworth poem I read with my students. By the wood line behind our house, the snow fell fast on the daffodils, as they startled the eye against the brown drab of the fallen leaves coating the forest floor. Raking leaves in the forest is futile, but I can't say it hasn't ever crossed my mind. It has. My urge is to clean it all away, but the forest is wide and deep; I couldn't ever accomplish my goal, so I've accepted it. The trees were budding and the flowering dogwoods lining our driveway were white as the snow.

A few days prior, it had felt like summer; the sun felt suddenly too warm in the sky, my spring clothes too heavy for the heat. Daffodils were surrounded by leaves and covered in snow, and the blooming dogwoods had snow on their branches, just days after the warning of summer heat. Spring met fall met winter met summer. The seasons were all jumbled and not at all blessing and releasing each other— one stretching its fingers into another, forever friends and enemies, all at the same time, much like the seasons in our own lives.

For much of my life, I've lived in Pennsylvania, a state with four distinct seasons. And while the shifting of the literal seasons can, at times, seem jarring to some, I've learned to see the holiness in each one. I love them all for different reasons and have come to see them as a way to see beauty everywhere and to honor life's gifts in the way they're revealed to us through the literal and metaphorical changing of the earth. I'm a four-season type of girl, but the concept hasn't been as easy for me when applied to life. While it might be easy for me to breathe and then bless and release the snow of the winter or the rain of the spring, it's not as easy for me in the shifting winds that make up this life. Quite honestly, those winds can sometimes leave me out of breath and on my knees.

Learning how to bless and release—to breathe and let go—isn't easy, but it's essential. My husband probably texts me the word *breathe* a few times a week and I joke that I'm going to get that tattooed on my arm. I might yet. For me, blessing and releasing is saying our thanks for people, situations, or things as they come to us and releasing them as they leave. Of course, that's easier said than done, but I see it as crucial for welcoming the blessings as they're given and releasing them when they shift, are taken away, or morph into something else. It's hard—downright impossible sometimes—no doubt, especially when it's not a thing at all but people we love, but so very much of life seems to be about letting go: letting go of the illusions of who you should be, phases you find yourself stuck in, houses you move in and out of, children as they move beyond your arms and venture into the world, and even loved ones who have walked away, or worse, passed away. None of it's easy.

When Matt was only around four years old, before

Maggie was born and before we moved to our current house now on the hill, I took Matt to see my childhood house, the one I grew up in and lived in for fourteen years, the one with the clearing back behind in the woods. By the time Matt and I took the drive, I was a thirty-four-year-old woman and I'd lived in about nine other homes, another state, and a different country, but I'm convinced our childhood homes remain steadfast.

My old house sits on a dirt road, a few miles off the main road. It had been almost two decades since I'd left, and since that time, I had only driven by it twice. My heart couldn't bear it, my connection to the land so strong it truly hurt. But I wanted Matt to know me better, for him to see where I came from. I wanted the boy I loved to know the place I loved. We drove back down the road, past a barn, that one where I used to stand on the rungs and talk to the cows. The barn looked different, its planks dark brown, almost black, the boards coming undone.

We parked in front of my old house and my eyes filled with tears. Matt didn't see them and started asking questions about my life there, trying to imagine his mama in the stream that's really just a creek and runs on the front of the property, trying to see me checking the mail at the end of the long driveway (one of my favorite things to do, as I was always waiting for a letter from my pen pal) or playing in the little orchard my dad had planted or in my mom's small garden she labored over on the hillside of red-clay dirt. Matt couldn't envision me there, though, and I started to cry because that bothered me most of all. My small boy couldn't see me there because the time had passed. To him, I was the mama who lived in a house in town with stained-glass windows and shiny floors. To him, I was the mama with pretty clothes and shoes, not the girl who lived there, on that dirt road, in the hills of the Allegheny Mountains of Appalachia, the girl who once fell into that creek in her coveted purple sweatshirt when the water overtook its banks during a flood. The girl who ran in the fields of wildflowers confidently, like she belonged there, *because* she belonged there, to the place but more importantly to herself. The black-eyed Susans were her very favorite.

As we took in the scene before us, tears rolled down my face at the memories. I wanted to get to the clearing way behind the house, the one tucked back in the woods on the hill, but I was with Matt and wasn't about to drag him through the field, over the creek, trespassing as we went. He couldn't see me and kept prattling about our house—the one we lived in then with his daddy, before Maggie was born and we moved to our own country home. As he continued, my head cleared and the fog of grief lifted. I wiped my face with the palm of my hand and turned and smiled at him. He smiled back and said, "Let's go home, Mama." It took his words to remind me my home was in a different place now. I said goodbye to the house, a final one, I thought, only to be repeated years later, but one I should've said way before that moment. I said a prayer for the people who lived there. I prayed for the house, the memory, my need to feel the way

I had years before, the girl I was then and was trying to be again, and then I released it, for the moment, anyway.

All these years later, my little family knows how important my childhood home is to me. One of the tags on my necklace was a gift from Mike when I signed the contract for this book. The latitude and longitude coordinates for that property are engraved on it. I know well where I came from and I don't ever want to forget, but now I have my own country home with my little family, and the idea of home is as important as ever. Blessing and releasing the homes we've lived in, for example, is a part of finding a holy everywhere. It isn't all confined to one place, of course. Holy, holy. It extends and stretches its hands across time and space. It is a time traveler, a connector, moving at lightning speed through the black universe, traveling in the warp of time and space.

⁊

At our house now, we always have music of some sort playing. One night, in the dead of winter, all four of us sat on the living-room floor, by the fire. The kids love to sing with us and it's become something we all like to do. Mike put on "Seven Bridges Road" by the Eagles and I was transported back to 1995 to the Outer Banks. My friend had come to the beach for the week with my family. She and I were close then, like sisters, and I was so happy to have an entire week with her. I was also dating Mike then, and coincidentally, his family was in Sandbridge, Virginia, a beach about two hours away. His best friend was with him and his family for the week. After getting permission from our parents, they came to see us for the day.

We all loaded up in Mike's mom's blue Ford Taurus and took a drive down the coast. I remember my friend's strawberry blond hair, a similar color to Maggie's now, blowing in the breeze of the opened windows. Mike had long hair that summer—the only time in his entire life—and his curls were the same as Maggie's. How odd to have seen her hair in front of me long before I even knew it. The Eagles' song came on and we belted it out. I'm not sure I'll ever forget that night in North Carolina—the warm air, the tanned skin, the air of possibility, being surrounded by three people I truly loved. And it connected to the moment with my little family, twenty-three years later, by the fire at our home in Pennsylvania through the song, through the people with the same hair color, through the understanding that the memory from that summer was somehow connected to that fireplace moment—the confirmation that as things change, people and moments can be connected, even as it all shifts and our lives shift with it. I think the best part about breathing, blessing, and releasing is that it can all come back to you, in ways you didn't imagine, as one phase of life morphs into another, one breath giving way to another, just like life.

∽

When we lived in Virginia Beach and I was starting out as a teacher, my summers off were spent on the Chesapeake Bay, at the oceanfront of the Atlantic, or by the pool with my fellow teacher friends. Back then, on those summer days, for the first time since childhood, I spent the days of summer however I wanted. I'd meet my friends by the water, carting my beach chair and a small cooler with mostly water or Diet Cokes, and maybe even some other drink to sip on. In my beach bag, I'd have magazines and books and a bag of pretzels. I carried pretzels everywhere in those days. My friends and I spent our days in our bikinis, soaking up carefree youth. Even as I've settled into new phases of life since then, I'd be lying if I told you I didn't miss the beach, the water, the humid air, the friends I had, and a metabolism that dealt well with an endless supply of nutritionless snack food.

When Mike finished his time in the navy, we moved away, and I mourned it. There was no blessing and releasing then. I'm a mountain girl at heart, but my love for the Chesapeake is true. There really isn't anything like the slow lapping water of the bay, and even writing about it, I miss it. It was the right move, though, painful as it was, and I've made friends, of course. We've had different adventures, and I've missed the kind of daily friendship where you sit all day by the water, sipping a Diet Coke, laughing. But I've spent too long of a time missing a stage of life that has passed.

Seasons passed, and I'd sit in my sister's pool, Matt in his little raft beside me, or occasionally at the beach on my summers off, his baby feet kicking with joy. Years later, Maggie's white eyelet hat shielded her baby head on the beach and I was content to sit with her in my lap, convinced of my place in the universe. I really was. But even as I lived in the moment, there were days I spent too much time dwelling on what once was.

But here's what I've learned, and it's helped me breathe, bless, and release: it all comes around, the days past, I mean, if we learn to let go. One flows into another, and suddenly, you find yourself not being needed by the poolside, or by the beach, or by the bay. The children are not there at all now, their own activities now a part of life, and I am sitting, not needed, for once, simply basking in the sun I forgot was so warm, simply sitting, which I'd almost forgotten how to do. My friend is in the chair beside me and I look in the cooler and there are two cans. I crack open one for her and one for me, and suddenly, it's the same—one season returning as another passes. And I smile at the way life circles back around, if just for a moment or an afternoon. Blessing and releasing allows it to be so.

◒◓

A few years ago, I was considering a new job. I hadn't exactly sought it out, but when I was approached about it, I really did pause. The job sounded perfect to the Kara I was in my twenties, back when I worked in more of an administrative role in a school, and I was intrigued. In fact, I strongly considered taking it if it was offered to me because I missed that kind of work: the leadership, talking to adults, and wearing high-heeled shoes! But in the back of my mind, I kept hearing, *This isn't who you are now.* I ignored it, though, and covered up the relatively new tattoos (gotten in the past few years) of the mountains, cross, and eagle I have on my wrists with bracelets and a watch, then put on a beautiful new suit and thought, *She's still there.*

I actually fought it—the idea that I'd changed, even though that very change was what I needed to find myself again. There was a very real part of me who wanted to abandon writing and our small-scale farming life to return to something that was perhaps more comfortable or at least proved, driven by results, more finite. The temptation was strong, the idea almost martyr-like, to give up on a dream of writing and the quiet life I love—maybe a coffee shop someday, like I'd always dreamed?—to make a switch to something that, in many ways, seemed easier to me, less emotional with less heartache and introspection.

Writing often feels too hard, too much, too emotional, too soul-revealing. I've been emotional as I've written much of this book, sometimes because what I say is painful or hard to remember but just as often because of the joy. And even that, the joy of the past, sometimes seems like too much to bear. It would be easier, truthfully, to bury my head in the sand, ignore my emotions like life has taught me to do (and I am unlearning, day by day), and go back to the pursuit of *being something more and doing more.* The pull of *that* is strong for me, even as this particular job was good *work,* essential work, work I admire and respect. *Work that must be done.* But, after much deliberation and soul-searching, I decided that it's just not the work for *me*, at least not now anyway. It's just not the season I'm in.

By learning to breathe, bless, and release, we can give in to the days we're *in.* If our decisions are rooted in what's real in the moment, perhaps that's how we get closest to the truest versions of ourselves. Sometimes that's an impossible thing to figure out. But what helped me was to think about what role brings out my truest self for the life I'm currently in. What fosters your strengths? What brings out sides of yourself you aren't proud of? What allows you to live a life that makes your soul sing? What allows you to serve in the best way? For me, these are the days of mothering, writing, and teaching. I accept it and release what *was* in order to pursue, fully, what is right *here.* And what's right here is pretty great.

Many of us fight the wisdom that comes with age (and, I believe, every age carries some wisdom) because it's more appealing to return to some stage of life when life seemed to be relatively easy. For me, that was my twenties and early thirties. It seemed easier to pretend to be someone I wasn't, trading out my interesting sterling silver jewelry for pearls, donating my Birkenstocks and swapping them for heels, buying a fancier car than I could maybe afford only because it made me feel like I "fit in" to an area so different from the dirt road I grew up on. I desperately wanted to be an insider, and I'd be a chameleon in order to be one, hiding the parts of myself that maybe didn't fit. As Mike and I moved multiple times in those years, I was in a constant state of *proving* and *hiding* myself instead of just *being* myself. It became a bit of an obsession: to impress the most, to be who I thought everyone wanted or expected me to be (when, really, maybe no one expected anything!). But now that whole charade is too much for me—the pace too tiring, the pretending just downright exhausting, the costume simply stifling.

I'm a country girl, just like I told my dad one day when I was four and begged him to take me on some sort of outdoor adventure he was going on. I savor watching my children ride their bikes in our driveway with a view of the mountains and talking to my students about books while I have a cup of hot tea in my hand. Last year, I bought a replica pair of the Birkenstocks I had donated almost twenty years before and I've started to wear overalls again. I love to hand-feed my chickens strawberries and look at the pink peonies outside my window. The cats wait for me to put food in the blue willow bowls my mom gave me and I actually talk to them like I did years ago to our cats at my childhood home. (Yes, my cats are fancy. Mike joked with me today that I need a bumper sticker that says "cat lady.") *It's all who I am.*

Writing, while hard, is *who I am now.* I'm not sure if it's how I'm to work in the world forever, but I'm willing to find out. Are you willing to find out where your passion will take you? Are you ready to see where it leads? Be brave if you can, or walk scared if it's all you can do. (Sometimes, it's all we can do.) I've walked scared so many times. But just take the steps. Breathing, blessing, and releasing allows us to find out about ourselves and our life paths. Of course, it's easier to walk away when things are hard or if we don't like where we are, but here's the thing I've learned: even when we walk away from places or things or people we love, we don't stop loving them, and it doesn't mean we are unhappy. It's just that we're walking down another path to another place or thing or person for a time.

In this house on the hill, each morning I walk from room to room, straightening beds, pulling sheets tight, smoothing out the wrinkles with my hands from the small child who left them. Even as they're safe and in school, there's something very comforting about my hands going over the memory of them on the sheets. It's like a prayer, the tracing of them. Since the school shootings in recent years, I have a hard time each day dropping off my kids at school—fear can get the best of me—but feeling the memory of them on the sheets is one way I've learned to breathe in, bless, and release. The sheets help. Small things often help us the most, I think.

On a night when the curtains are open in my bedroom and the lights are off, I can see the stars from my spot in our bed. Years ago, I never would have even noticed. But this kind of thoughtful noticing has become the way I look at most everything now. Last night, I looked over my sleeping husband's head at the faraway star in the bottom right-hand windowpane. As bright as day, it shone, its sparkle impossible to dull—the light in the indigo sea of the dark midnight sky, stretching endlessly, infinite, fathomless. The sky was so dark but the star twinkled, no matter the darkness. She didn't care. Nothing could stop her from shining.

The house was quiet with my sleeping family and I stared at the star until my eyes closed again and I, too, drifted into the indigo sea of the sky, thinking of myself as the dreamer ready to dream of a different life but then realizing my dreams won't be any better than this bed, on this night, in this house, looking out the window at this star. You see, seeing this star helped me realize that I'm *right where I'm to be* because the star is *right where it is to be*. It's *all* by design. God has his hand in it all.

ॐ

Simple things can remind and tether us. Simple things, like the making of oatmeal even, can tether us. And it's oatmeal season again, somehow. I wait for the teakettle to roar as I put yesterday's shoes away, discarded carelessly by the back door. There are always so many shoes, and even as that annoys me (it really does), I'm grateful for the shoes and my people who wear them. Matt eats two packets of oatmeal now and even though I offer many things for breakfast, that's his choice. But it's breezy here and cool and oatmeal seems like the natural choice for a day like today.

The earliest leaves are falling fast on our roof, a stark orange contrast against the blue of the metal, and the dog's favorite thing to do is to sit in the chair by my bathroom window and watch the leaves swirl. Frances sits with her head over the back, her nose out of the opened window, and she stares, enchanted by the dance of the leaves. I mix Matt's oatmeal, carefully adding extra brown sugar, just the way he likes it. It thickens to a hearty weight, the boiling water swelling the oats, the goodness filling the air on an otherwise drab morning. It's the getting of the breakfast this morning that keeps me going, the warm bowl in my hand as I deliver it to his bedroom because he asked if he could please sleep a bit longer before getting up and getting ready for school. He's older and sleeping later. The oatmeal season is here again, with the leaves all aflutter. I take one final whiff of the maple and brown sugar oatmeal and I exhale, blessing and releasing, as I open his bedroom curtain to the fall waiting outside, shedding its light right on the still sleeping, still summer-bleached head of my son.

CHAPTER 7

Walk with Me

We all need one another, much and often.

—CHARLOTTE PERKINS GILMAN,
WOMEN AND ECONOMICS

M om, I'll walk with you," Matt said one September day
as we were walking to pick apples in the lower part of
our yard. Maggie and Mike drove down in the little ATV my
dad sometimes leaves here so we can haul the apples back to
the house for sorting. And while there is room for us all in
it, I said I'd walk and Matt said, "I'll walk with you, Mom.
Here, hold my hand." As he grabbed my hand, I said, "I'll
walk with you too."

In the eighties, in the rural community I grew up in,

it wasn't uncommon for friends to stop in and sit with us on the porch, sitting at the small table my mom had on one end, opposite from the porch swing. There generally wasn't a phone call beforehand and certainly no text messages. People just showed up, and my mom would throw on a pot of coffee, and we'd just pass the evening together. The parents sipped coffee on the porch while the kids played. I remember the ease of those days.

My husband tells similar stories of hand churning ice cream with people who traveled down the road to his own house, not too far from my own. His parents would call over the neighbors to share in the bounty at their picnic table. It was rural life in the eighties at its best, but I think we can have this now, wherever we are, if we try to realize the gifts of our people and take the time to really *see* them—in person.

These days, it seems that people plan coffee and lunch dates, making an electronic appointment in their iPhone calendars weeks in advance. I do it too. Sometimes it feels like we've lost what the gift of real community can mean—the gift it is to sit with people (literally, metaphorically, spiritually). But one step in seeing the holiness all around us, I think, is taking the time to build community and to feel the healing powers of it. In a harried life, it's hard, but I think it's pretty essential. After all, we all want to belong somewhere and with someone.

On a random Sunday evening, we had friends over for a rather impromptu dinner. We're last-minute people, in general, so my invites usually come at the last minute. My husband had baked a loaf of his famous bread (it's the best, really), and as I sat there, at our long dining room table, I couldn't help but notice the holy moment—the breaking of bread with friends. I was reminded of the scripture verse I love about breaking bread and eating with joyful hearts (Acts 2:46). That night, we did eat together with joyful hearts. Sacred Sunday looked a lot like friends around the dinner table. It smelled a lot like freshly baked bread and it sounded like kids playing. Breaking bread—literally—is what Sunday has come to mean to me. Our home practice is a sort of church—right here over homemade bread, messy and loud with too many carbs and tea and kids coloring on my long dining room table—and it's one of the things I love most. These are moments we can see holiness—when we invite people to our table and into our homes as Jesus really intended. I've seen this at work in various ways, in many metaphors, and one instance from the summer of 1999 really sticks out even now, all these years later.

It was a hot summer day, a day so hot, my northern lungs felt like they couldn't breathe through the thickness of a humidity I wasn't used to then. I was walking and applying for jobs in Virginia Beach, living there before I left for my study-abroad trip to England that fall, desperate to act more adult than I felt. I remember well what I was wearing—a burnt-orange broomstick dress, so popular then, my hair pulled back in a long braid. After applying for a waitressing job at a restaurant—an ultra-hip place where people colored on the walls and tables and where I knew, instinctively, I wouldn't fit in—I left the darkness of the restaurant and was assaulted by the power of the sun.

I didn't have my sunglasses and sighed heavily as I dug for my list of places to apply in my floral embroidered bag, the one I loved and wish I still had. I needed a job or else I'd be forced to admit I really wasn't an adult. I'd need to move back home with my parents and return to the job I had at Barnes & Noble. I really didn't want to do any of that. I spotted a health food store and a coffee shop beyond the parking lot exit from the restaurant, and I made a quick decision and walked toward the coffee shop to grab a mocha with the last three dollars crumpled up at the bottom of my bag. It was a frivolous way to spend money; I knew that, but in many ways, I guess I've always believed coffee solves most problems. It always seemed to help my parents when I was small.

When I opened the door to the coffee shop, I immediately loved everything about it—the copper-top tables, the miniature camelback sofa (which I now have in my house), the bookshelves filled with old books and trinkets, the energy and spirit. Photos lined the other spaces and two women were behind the counter, taking orders, clearly enjoying their work and, most likely, their friendship. I remember even now how happy they looked, the coffee shop's own Thelma and Louise. I ordered my mocha and waited my turn, thinking about the ridiculousness it was even *to be* in Virginia Beach at twenty and to be with my boyfriend (Mike!) who was stationed in Norfolk and who would be deployed for much of the summer. Resolute in my decision on the outside, my inner turmoil was pretty extreme, but I was too scared to admit that maybe I'd made a mistake.

As thoughts raced through my head, one of the women behind the bar asked me how my day was going and where I was from. Words spilled out—"I'm from Pennsylvania, looking for a job"—and my eyes filled with tears. She just looked at me and smiled before she said, "Well, I'm hiring." There was no Help Wanted sign posted, and her friend making my mocha looked surprised when she said, "Can you come back tomorrow around nine-ish and we'll see what kind of fit we are together?" Her "nine-ish" appealed to me, the English major artist, the free spirit I still wanted to be.

I worked there, on and off, for a few years, and some of the best times of my transitional years—the years between childhood and adulthood—were spent there behind the bar, making coffees or writing in my journal when it wasn't busy. I wrote pages and pages, in journal after journal, over the years. The owner encouraged me to write and I did, in that little shop a block from the ocean. I met people who encouraged me and taught me the gift of community, welcoming me into their homes for dinner and giving me hugs when I needed them. I learned there how to create a community wherever I am, a valuable lesson that has followed me. Now, years later, I'm blessed to say I've done that in this town in Pennsylvania and I've learned that, sometimes, gifts are revealed in these ordinary things like making coffee—or even in doing laundry.

෧

During one of her visits, my mom helped me rearrange my living room and sort through toys in the playroom. She knew I had an ongoing battle with organization, especially laundry, and she offered a solution: get a laundry sorter. After years and years of struggling, I snickered and said, "Mom, I doubt a laundry sorter will solve this problem." The very next day, I took my mom's advice and went in search of a laundry sorter. I found one and brought it home and my husband put it together, chuckling. Would this finally stop our fight with the piles of laundry? Neither one of us thought it would. But I faithfully sorted, doing a load of laundry every time a color bin was full.

Weeks before this, I was told that thoughts are ever changing and I was encouraged to remind myself that my anxious thoughts are, after all, only thoughts, not reality. They're fleeting, like the fog I've grown to love so much. Of course, I love metaphor, so I try to envision my worried thoughts and convoluted fears as the fog rising from the mountains, never permanent, always changing. Even so, I truly didn't think the words would help me, just like I doubted the laundry sorter would. But just as I sorted laundry, sock after sock, I faithfully said those words every time a worry arose.

And here's the thing: both things actually helped me. These small steps and simple efforts made a difference! Step by step and day by day, I did loads of laundry. One at a time, I emptied the bins into the washer, put them in the dryer, and folded them on my bed. I walked them to each room and put them away in drawers and on hangers in closets. And guess what? It worked. The laundry sorter worked (when I used it)! Why hadn't I done it before? Why hadn't *I* thought of this?

Similarly, each time a worry or fear reached me, I simply said, "These are only thoughts," and I did my best to move on. My issues with anxious thoughts are perhaps long-lasting, but with a few words, at times, I was able to keep them from infecting me or torturing me as they'd done in the past. I never really would have believed it, but it was in the words and suggestions of others—*these gifts of my people*—that I found some semblance of peace from time to time, both at home with the endless laundry and in my own head. Still, others can remind us of parts of ourselves we might have forgotten.

For our sixteenth wedding anniversary, Mike and I went away with friends who were also celebrating sixteen years of marriage. We randomly picked a town on one of the smaller lakes in the Finger Lakes, and with almost no planning at all in terms of our actual trip (we did plan for children and animals, of course), we loaded up in their SUV and made the three-hour trip. I felt young again—like the carefree days I once had years before. For three days, I cackled (and there are unflattering pictures to prove it!). In one store, it was over funny coasters—until I cried. Then I had this revelation, this memory: *Yes, Kara, you love to laugh and you love*

people who help you to be lighthearted. Your most favorite
people make you laugh.

One afternoon while in the Finger Lakes, my friend
and I were sitting outside on Adirondack chairs while our
husbands played cornhole. We simply sat and talked and,
mostly, we laughed. As we were sitting there, the bright sun
smiling on us, the sky clear, the breeze so very fine, she said,
"Kara, there's a bald eagle!" She knows I love eagles, as I
have one tattooed on my wrist. And truly, who doesn't love
watching one soar? We watched it fly low and land on a
tree in the field across from us, and it seemed to be there to
remind me to pay attention to this moment, just as the eagle
did months before in the river. This time, it brought another
reminder, just like last time. I was reminded of this: I'm not
alone. Yes, I love to laugh. Yes, our people are a gift from
God and he truly *wants us to be happy.* Despite the suffering
we're sure to encounter, he wants us to laugh and the gifts of
our people are actually direct gifts from him.

There is a tradition at the school where I teach. Every year,
the night before graduation, the school hosts a special senior
dinner. Every senior is able to choose a teacher to invite to
the dinner. Most years, I've been invited, but in a recent year,
I was not. I wasn't the only teacher not invited, and even as I
knew this to be true, I'd be lying if I told you it didn't sting,
if just a little; it did. I allowed the feeling to linger a bit longer

than I should have before getting on with my day, my disappointment mostly behind me. Teaching, while rewarding on many days, is sometimes thankless and I felt discouraged.

Later that very day, I received an email from a parent thanking me for my work with her daughter that year. I read her words and started to cry, consistently amazed by the connections, the coincidences, the intercessions that stack up time after time, day after day. I notice them now and say my thanks for the email and the reminder that while sometimes I feel like what I'm doing doesn't at all matter, it does to someone. Please remember this: even when we feel like what we do doesn't matter, it *does*. It really does. *You matter.* And our people are sometimes the best reminders, as Matt once reminded me.

In the car on the way home from school, Matt described his relationship with his best friend. He said, "We're just such good friends. We're like brothers." He pointed up through the seats and said, "Do you see how that road curves up ahead? If he were all the way down there, I'd go to him. I wouldn't just wait here for him to catch up to me. Good friends don't do that. I'd walk all the way there so I could walk with him. That's the kind of friends we are. I'd never let him walk alone. Plus, he's like my brother."

My son's words were literal, but in them, I think he has the crux of friendship figured out: *we walk to the people we love*. Sometimes, that might look like a daddy setting up a little game with red Solo cups and dollar-store prizes for his four-year-old daughter who had lost game after game at the amusement park. Other times, it might look like my mom washing her best friend's hair before she died, when she was sick from her chemo treatment. We never let our people walk alone. It's not always easy; this I understand, but maybe it could get easier.

Years ago, I had a friend tell me we could no longer be friends because we thought of things so differently. That crushed me because I thought she was one of my people, even if we had different opinions. We can love people who think differently or are different from us, of course, but I'm sure you have similar stories. Instead of focusing on our differences, what if we found even just a small piece of common ground? Could it be that simple? I think so, and I always look to nature for lessons.

My parents now live in a small town about thirty minutes from my house and, for years, they have had chickens in a small coop in the backyard. In what we assume was a mink or weasel massacre, all but one of their three chickens were killed. Henrietta, an old hen who doesn't lay eggs anymore, was the only one left next to the feathers of her longtime friends. The image makes me sad every time I think about it. In all the years my parents had had the coop and their flock, nothing had ever gotten in until that fateful night. Henrietta was lonely and sad and my parents brought her to our house to join our flock, thinking she'd be happier with friends. While we have so many different varieties of birds, she looks different because she's a Barred Rock. Her feathers are black and white and her comb is the most vibrant red. She's one of our prettiest birds and is my favorite hen now. Henrietta wandered around our property and the flock didn't accept her right away. Some of the other hens even pecked her before they went off in their two groups. Imagine seeing your family killed and then going for refuge in a new place and being rejected. It's too hard to think about, really, but there's a powerful lesson here. Henrietta stayed close to me and I talked to her softly. She followed me. Mike gave me a piece of corn and I lay in the grass with it. She walked around me before coming very close and eating from my hand. It was just a piece of corn—just a hand, outstretched—just food for the hungry and the sad. It wasn't that hard to do. It's not that hard to do. Maybe it's just one small step at a time? Maybe it's just in the reaching of hands? Eventually, the flock did accept Henrietta and now they can be seen sharing a tomato snack together from time to time or huddled together in the coop when the night falls.

Tonight as I type this chapter, the stars are shining so brightly. When I looked up at them before I came in tonight, the universe seemed to slow just for a second. The beauty of the open sky made it easy to imagine there were no wars, no division, no *us versus them* mentality, even in my own head. Maybe if we all stopped worrying about what separates us, we could see it this way. Could we build a bridge, create a pass through the mountains that divide us? Like the stars, maybe we could just join together, for the common good—coming together to light up the darkness. Maybe we can start in our own community, in our own yards, with our own people and the relationships we have. God calls us to walk and sit together, and a holiness is revealed everywhere if we can only learn how.

For much of my adult life, I dreamed of a large dining room with a big tavern table—large enough to fit the big family I always wanted. When we came and saw our current home for the first time, Mike whispered in my ear, "It's your dream space, Karrie." And so, I am lucky enough to have that big tavern table now; my friend's dad built it for us when we moved in. But really, I always have had the room, if not at a literal table.

No matter the size of our tables, we can make room wherever we sit. Tables, like hearts, can make room for people who have different opinions or beliefs or who look, worship, or love differently than we do. Isn't that what makes the table so special? The laughter and chaos, the discussions and maybe even the occasional disagreement, loud and right there, right over the mashed potatoes or the baked corn (my favorite!)? It happens at my table, for sure. Holy moments can be messy, but the mess can also reveal the gifts. It's not all hallowed halls and candles, hushed prayers and quiet reflection. Sometimes it's messy and loud and altogether chaotic. Sometimes there's even yelling! Yes! There's a lot of chaos in my house (and I even have a Chaos Coordinator t-shirt), but guess what? Chaos can be holy! Once we understand that, we are free to see it all around, even in skinned knees and tears.

In early June, Maggie fell as she ran down the driveway, the dog on her heels. When I went to check on her, I knelt down to find she had a skinned knee and a stray tear on her face. As I got back up, I looked up and saw our cherry tree. It was only the first week of June, so it wasn't really cherry-picking time, but one was looking redder than the others, so I plucked it from the tree, the first cherry of the year. Usually we ceremoniously do this, but instead I pulled it from the tree and put it in her small hand to cheer her up. She smiled and wiped away her tear, as she, too, seemed to remember the ceremony of the year before and her need to include her people. Even if she didn't remember, instead of popping it in her mouth, she said, "We need to show Daddy and Matt." We walked to them, the not ripe but *good enough* cherry in her fingers. She showed them and they smiled and she put the cherry in her mouth. It wasn't perfect—the cherry—but the moment? It was holy and a reminder of holy being everywhere, especially right in my own people, who love one another enough to share the beating red-heart beauty of June's very first cherry.

CHAPTER 8

This Beating, Tattered Heart

Mama, God gave us our hearts to love people.

—MAGGIE, AGE THREE

It was mid-April, but it was still cold out, even in the cathedral, even in my wool coat. I sat down by my father behind another father and his two teenage boys. As we waited for the service to begin, the church filled, its hallowed halls filled with whispers, the candles casting a perfect glow on the pillars, the shadows dancing from the flicker. Right before the service began, a woman quickly ran in and sat with the father and the two boys. I could tell she was the mother and wife of the trio in front of me; they clearly were a family.

Because she came in late, she sat behind a marble pillar and couldn't see the altar. The father kept glancing at her, trying to catch her eye, but she didn't look at him. She seemed flustered, maybe annoyed. As the service began, he quickly walked to her and whispered to her that he wanted her to be able to see. His voice was soft and low, but I could hear it. His sons must have also heard him because they smiled as the father gave up his spot and the mother replaced it, a blond beside her two dark-as-night-haired sons. The youngest looked up—ever so slightly, as he was almost as tall as she was. His look had adoration in it and I saw it, the look almost bringing me to tears because I can only hope my own son looks at me that way when he's a teenager. The father, now in his wife's spot behind the pillar, sang during church, an example to his sons of how things are done.

In the giving of his spot, I was reminded that we give of ourselves to our people even if it means that we give up something of ourselves—a view, a position. That's just what I saw when the father gave up his view of the altar, of the table, of the feast of the Lamb. He didn't need to see it; he felt it, and as I watched the scene play out in front of me, I felt the holiness, too—more than the ritual, the liturgy, the flicker of the candles on the recesses of the pillars, more than the hands held out in prayer or the hand-holding or the bread or wine.

Later, when it was time to kneel, this man and one of his sons didn't have a kneeler because the pew was behind the pillar. The cold marble would have been made harder and colder, I imagine, by the frigid chill of the air from the side door not too far away from where we all were. Without hesitation, contemplation, or any signs of internal negotiation, the father knelt first, and without words, his son knelt, too, giving his mom the space on the kneeler. Their backs tall, their knees to the marble, their heads down in supplication. It was beautiful.

The image of them reminded me that relationships were never promised to be easy for any of us. I mean, when things are going well and life seems so very good, they can seem easy. When things are going our way and there's no pain and suffering on our path, sure—we walk straight ahead. Easy. But, as I knelt on my own kneeler, in my own pew, I was reminded, again, that sometimes, it feels a lot like cold marble on tired knees, Aprils that just won't turn into the real spring we crave, candles that blow out from the frigid air. When we suddenly have that understanding, maybe it can get easier? Love is often like cold marble on our tired knees, and yet we feel it, pain and all, and we can find an everywhere holy in it.

That's real-life love—what I saw in the church that day. Real-life love is hard work and commitment, failure and triumph. Don't let people tell you things need to be effortless to be worth having. It's one of the biggest lies, I believe, and why many of us flee from anything that forces us to see a new perspective, dig deep, or sit in some sort of discomfort with those we love. Love of any kind requires more than just the good times. Love requires these kneeling-on-marble kinds of moments; it requires the wading through the muck and the mire, the hard talks and the revelation of even harder truths, and the ability to begin again, if that's what's the best in the end. And it might not always be.

Shortly after witnessing this man kneel on cold marble, I was in church again and my prayer was to strengthen my marriage and to remind us of one another. It had been almost sixteen years since we married and so much had changed. Life tends to do that to our relationships, doesn't it? We've moved; we've graduated with various degrees; we've gotten promotions; we've gained and lost friends; we've been disappointed in some ways and felt like we've failed in others. We've won some and we've lost some. But I had been worrying that we'd forgotten who we were together. So I just kept praying, *Please remind us of why we're together. Please strengthen this marriage.*

We left church and came home to a day full of various jobs around the house, mostly avoiding the gaze of the other. At the time, the pace of our lives made connecting difficult, and in that particular season, I was in charge of a fundraiser with a girlfriend for our sons' school and I wanted to find some Saint Patrick's decor in the freshly cleaned basement to decorate with.

All the boxes we never unpacked from moving almost two years before were mixed in with the various boxes of holiday decorations. I searched and searched for the decorations, but I couldn't find them. Box after box, I searched, until I stumbled upon a box full of photo albums, and in it was our wedding album, which I thought I had lost in one of our moves. There was also an album my husband made for me on our first wedding anniversary, complete with poetry he wrote to me and photos of us from our first dance together way back in 1992. I had forgotten he ever wrote me poetry or that he wrote at all. And it was like a confirmation of a prayer answered, a reminder that yes, maybe we're still who we were together.

That night, I had a dream that my small family—Mike, Matt, Maggie, and me—were at my old childhood home, the one I've talked about here, but it looked different somehow than it actually ever was. The creek was much wider and much more beautiful than it ever was, trees hanging over it like a canopy. Still, I knew where I was. My soul knew the song of the place. It was sunny but the sun was just peeking through the trees, making beautiful and varied designs on the water that was sparkling under its rays. Dancing—that's what the water almost looked like it was doing as it fell over the rocks, rushing in some areas but never too quick to knock anyone down.

My husband and I were fighting in the dream—a continuation of what had been real life for us at the time, a marriage edging two decades—but we stopped in awe of the scene before us. There were two fawns in the water, just standing, staring at my children as if they knew them as they made their way upstream to them. The fawns waited for them and allowed the kids to pet them. They were beautiful: the fawns with their big white spots, and my children, with their bright eyes and wild hair—Maggie's curls all unruly and Matt's full head of thick hair, all messy and standing straight up. Maggie scooped up one of the fawns in her arms and it was as big as she was, but somehow she had the strength to carry it. Her brother smiled with his arms outreached, just in case she fell, just in case she dropped her load. Like in real life, his arms were support if she needed them. They walked toward us, joyful, happy, content. We turned to one another and my husband grabbed my hand as we walked toward them, sure of nothing other than the love of this family of *ours*, the one we built together, despite the odds. The dream reminded me of what matters; I've learned dreams can remind us of the everywhere holy right in front of us, as can everyday moments in the kitchen.

On Good Friday of that year, I hugged Mike and kind of jokingly said, "Think we'll make it?" And he kissed my head and said, "Certainly." We hugged and Maggie came running. Her brother looked up from his book and walked over quickly. We all hugged and it was prayer personified, life in check and balance and *all is well*, if just for a moment. We stood and embraced and I rubbed my son's arm with one hand and Maggie's head with another and Mike breathed deeply into my hair. We just stood like that, longer than I thought we would or the kids would. Then we broke and

Mike looked at me with just a glimmer of a tear in his eyes and the kids smiled and walked off and he said, "That never gets old. None of that." No, no it doesn't.

⌒

That spring, I was so fixated on the tulips as they popped up in our flower beds. Despite snow only weeks prior, they bloomed in the splendor I've grown accustomed to—shades of red and yellow mostly, but there were a few purples scattered about. Like the daffodils a few weeks ahead of them, they reminded me of life. And I was reminded that nature, just like children, will always guide us if we let it. People, life, and flowers usually end up blossoming after the cold passes. I've found this to be true for me, countless times over.

Mike planted the red tulips for me and the color of them against the very green grass stunned me when they bloomed. He knew how much I loved them and took a picture with his phone and texted it to me. And in that gesture, I was reminded of something else: relationships of the heart seem like this to me—a cycle of seasons, but always *whispering holy* if we listen closely enough.

Sometimes relationships go through their own falls, where parts of them seem like they are dying. Slowly, like the leaves that fall, marriages sometimes have their own falling leaves—disagreements, financial troubles, health issues, just to name a few. When you're stuck in the fall of a marriage or partnership, it can feel hopeless—all aflutter, and the sure things you thought you had all nailed down and secure blow away with one swift movement of the breeze's arm. But the leaves are so very beautiful as they fall and you know that the trees will only be bare for a time. So you wait.

Winter comes and it's quiet. Brooding and cold and all you want to do is huddle under a blanket by your fireplace. But still, there's the snow, right outside your window, falling in a beautiful display—glistening, white, covering fences and time and *all of it.* You see the beauty is still very much alive even if the grass isn't, and somehow it's just so stunning. You take a deep breath of that cold air, the kind that clears your nostrils, and you get out the shovels and you dig out, creating paths back to one another, wearing your snow boots to keep your feet warm and dry, knowing *warm air is on its way. You know it. You've been here before. You're no stranger.* You hold hands to keep them warm and you wait.

And then the snow melts and the creek becomes so very alive with the extra water—*gushing*! I say to the kids and I spread my arms wide and they laugh—it's so loud now. I can hear it from inside the house and I love the sound. The grass gets greener by the day and the daffodils bloom, despite the lingering snow, despite the ominous clouds. I'm amazed at all the sudden green of the fields and mountains and there are days I simply live to breathe in the musky air from the freshly cut grass. And then, there's the red tulip. It's so red. There's the photo and someone who knows that nature is one of my favorite gifts. To be seen in nature or thought of when seeing God's beauty is the greatest compliment to me.

And so I smile and the red, crinkled-edge tulip is like my heart—vibrant and imperfect. So I go on. So *you* go on.

Summer takes her cue and it's really warm with the summer storms you've grown used to. And it's all so beautiful—*all of it*. The rain clears and the rainbows appear. You remember God's promise and what your Meemom told you about rainbows—how they're the sign from Pop-Pop that he's around. And you remember this about marriage, just like they did, just like your parents did: it really, really is seasonal. It edges and curves, with its ups and downs. And yes, maybe it doesn't always, can't always, or *shouldn't always* work out for everyone, but as for you, well, you're not ready to walk away, so you'll keep trying, right in the ordinary life of making coffee, even.

It was midafternoon and the day had been full already. Mike was tired; I could tell when he came in for his gloves and so I put on a pot of coffee. Books of all sorts and journals are some of the greatest gifts to me and of course I love a good cup of coffee, but coffee is Mike's *love language*. Truly, if his heart spoke, it would speak just like that, in red hushed whispers, its heart-hot breath smelling like coffee. I don't know anyone who loves coffee more than Mike. It's something I've worried about for a while—his coffee consumption—but truth be told, I was tired too. I grabbed the grinder and the bag of beans.

He loves whole-bean coffee and rarely buys it already ground. Each morning, while the house is asleep, the grinder can be heard, the waft of beans coming up the stairs to our bedroom, beckoning, pulling me from my sleep and our bed and down the stairs to him, standing there with the coffee grinder. Carefully, I poured the ebony beans into the grinder, a few overflowing. The smell overtook me as each bean fell into the grinder. I put the lid on it, the sound overpowering me, the smell a welcomed one. I carefully scooped out the coffee grounds and put them in the filter. I filled the coffeepot with water, poured it slowly into the coffee maker, focused on the water as it spilled, clean and clear, into the reservoir. I turned it on and listened to the popping sound of the water. I stood like that, my one leg crossed in front of the other, my hand on my hip, and I waited, fixated, for the coffee to percolate, watching it as it fell into the pot, brown drips coming quick.

He walked in again from outside and peeked around the back hall to me standing there in front of the coffee maker. He looked at me standing there, his blue eyes I love made bluer by the sun creeping in from the front door, and then sniffed the air, coffee wafting, his favorite scent, and he smiled. Maggie, then only three years old, told me that very same morning, "Mama, God gave us our hearts to love people." Profound and true. And while life is heavy sometimes and relationships sometimes hard, coffee was the way I showed love that day, a simple gesture returned with a smile, little things we all can do. Other days it's been him walking to me from across a crowded room.

ҩ

I help my students organize the prom at the school where I teach. Before the birth of our own children, Mike always came to the prom to help me chaperone, but for years he hadn't and instead stayed home and put our kids to bed. Last year, with children happily planted with their grandparents, he joined me to chaperone. Mostly we took care of various details and were often in different areas of the venue, but at one point, an Ed Sheeran song came on and I texted him to come and dance with me. I was sixteen again, briefly, waiting for him to walk through the door to me. He didn't reply to my text, but when I looked up, he was walking through the door toward me, just like I remember him doing when I was sixteen at the prom in 1995. He walked toward me, almost completely gray-haired now, and I quietly gave thanks for my marriage. We danced and I remembered, small steps reminding me of all the small steps toward one another instead of away from one another that have made this relationship stand the test of time, day by day. The small steps have made all the difference for us in the end, like the planting of flowers, roots all deep in the ground, reminding us of the roots we have with one another.

When we moved to our current home, I was very sad about all the flowers I'd be leaving behind. There were so many beautiful flowers, many that Mike and my mom dug up from her garden, replanted there by him. Knowing how much I loved them, he dug up a few peony bushes from the garden and planted them here at our new home. For the past two years, in early June they've bloomed, bright pink and vibrant, reminding me that love is sometimes shown in simple ways—flowers dug up in the heat of the summer, moved in buckets, and planted in the ground. Every June, they remind me of my marriage, how its petals have fallen, its leaves have wilted, but it always blooms again if tended to and cared for.

☙

We had celebrated our sixteenth anniversary weeks before with our friends in the Finger Lakes, so when we woke up to rain on the actual day, I assumed we'd just stay home. Upbeat, my husband kissed me on the forehead and gave me a cup of coffee. The past year hadn't been at all easy for me, for us, so he was determined to celebrate the day, the prayed-for and received renewal of life—mine and ours together. He told the kids and me to dress in hiking clothes and meet him downstairs. I smiled and, despite the worries of deadlines, I dressed and we loaded into the car. He surprised us with a trip to a local state park, one about thirty minutes away that boasts a swinging bridge, a waterfall, and a balancing rock. We hiked in the rain, the forest the comfort and protection we needed from the drops. Hardly getting wet at all, we hiked, holding the hands of our children and smiling at the joy the hike gave them.

I caught Mike looking at me a few times when the kids stared in amazement at some God-given wonder, and we looked at our children as the God-given wonder they are to us. In the past year, that hike in the rain was a bright moment for me, a revelation of sorts, that no matter what we're given, it's our choice how to live. Yes, it rained, but we have choices about how we treat the things beyond our control, like weather. It's only weather, after all, and even in the dark and gloomy rain of an end-of-June day, we hiked. As we hiked and climbed up the rudimentary rock stairs, I prayed. I prayed in gratitude, silent and small prayers, little ones that filled the air. The golden snail we found, nestled in a leaf roll on a moss rock with the brilliant green of ferns all over, was a reminder that, everywhere, there are holy signs. The tiny mice, scampering and scurrying, were signs that life goes on, in small ways. The children with me, confirmation that I am loved, for if I wasn't, how could I ever be given such a gift? The husband walking alongside me, the childhood friend who has become the man I spend my life with, was the reminder that while life and love aren't always easy, we just keep walking together and toward one another, as hard as it can be.

All around me and for as long as I can remember, I've watched couples struggle from time to time, and the only thing I've learned is this: marriage is sometimes hard (sometimes even *painstakingly* hard) work. That's been true for me and others I know. Some people will act like it's not, and maybe in various seasons of life, it's not much work. But in the end, marriage seems to me to be like a garden. You must tend to it or it will be overgrown with weeds of all kinds and poisons aplenty. Throughout my own marriage, we have realized we had some tending to do. Sure, we'd kept up over the years in some of the ways, but our garden was amuck with poisons and weeds and we simply couldn't find time to tend it. With two children with activities of their own, our jobs, a writing career I was trying to get off the ground, various hardships, the renovation of two houses, and the tending of animals and real-life gardens, our relationship was dead last and it was showing. We had a choice. Allow the weeds to take over and close the garden or roll up our sleeves and get our hands dirty. We chose to do the latter.

We chose to spend some time alone, regularly if possible. Yes, we're lucky to have parents who kept the kids for a few days so we could go away with friends to celebrate our wedding anniversary (the first-ever trip like that since we'd become parents!) and who help out in other ways. But we also kept a list of vetted and responsible babysitters. We set aside a bit of money to go out here and there—nothing fancy, and mostly we just met for an hour for lunch and talked. At first, we had lists of things to talk about because during the busiest times of our lives, we could rarely fit in entire sentences with one another. But, eventually, we took back our space, and the time alone was crucial for us.

If you can't spare the money for a sitter, I understand! Consider joining forces with a couple interested in doing the same and child-share on date nights. One week, you watch their kids for two hours for free while they have two hours alone and the next week, they watch your kids. There are many ways to accomplish this goal. Don't be discouraged.

And remember: it is good for your children to be with other people sometimes too!

There will be judgment, perhaps, in taking back parts of our lives from parenthood. But, while many of us are parents first and foremost these days (and *blessed* for it, yes), there is nothing wrong with being a person or a couple again. Listen to me: nothing is wrong with keeping your relationships alive and spending some time alone. There is nothing wrong with keeping *yourself alive* by taking time for you. Repeat that if you have to. At first I had to, but now I believe it with every fiber of my being.

Others will understand the need to work on these areas. A friend started her own date nights with her husband, walking to a trivia night while a babysitter kept her kids for a few hours. She and I had coffee together, sans kids, here and there because we made a point to. It was a priority. Listen, I'm not talking about running away to Europe for a month with your spouse (although that would be pretty cool in many ways!) or taking off to New York City for a girls' weekend with your best friends (although that would also be fun!); I'm talking about carving out some time to keep your relationships alive. One of the best things we can give our children are relationships of all kinds worthy of imitation. Of course, that comes in many ways, but I hope my children have the blessing of friends that I do or that they look at their spouses the way I sometimes do at mine.

One night I watched Mike walk toward the house, short-haired from his new haircut—a military cut I remember well—and almost totally gray, the white patch on the top of his head glowing in the gloom of the rainy afternoon. He took a drag of his cigar, a habit I disdain, smashed it on the retaining wall, and flicked his cigar beyond the flower bed, past the pink peonies he transplanted for me. The grass was wet, and after all these years I knew the cigar would be fine, discarded in the backyard and back by the tree line. He walked confidently to the house, shoulders back, unaware of my eyes looking beyond my computer and out the window at him.

For a minute, I saw the Mike of my early twenties. It's always strange to me when that happens—the time traveling that can happen simply by looking at a face, I mean. The way we can be transported simply by someone's smile or eyes or, in this case, the short haircut and the flick of a cigar. Against the backdrop of this life, I saw him in the previous ones. He was walking on the brick walkway here at our house in Pennsylvania, but I remember him walking on a dock to me one summer we took his old maroon Jeep CJ-7 he loved to Manteo, North Carolina. He had walked away from me to smoke because I've never liked it, and as he walked down the dock and returned to me, he flicked his cigarette into a trash can, one that still had the cigarette sand top they all used to have. I remember it like it was yesterday, but it was almost two decades ago now. I remember looking at him, slightly annoyed, but there was something in his walk and in his eyes that made me soften. And my holy, tattered, and beating heart whispered then and it whispers now, in the people God gave us to love. Who did God give your imperfect, sometimes tattered, beating heart to love? It might feel like a hard question, but often, the answer is simple. I just try to remember Maggie's words: "God gave us our hearts to love people," and now I know—hearts can expand, changing shape and color, beating fast or slow.

Mike looked at me while I was driving as the kids slept in the back seat. I could feel his eyes on me in the dark, the glow of the headlights enough for me to be able to see his face. I glanced quickly at him and he was staring at me, his eyes soft, a cup of coffee in his hand. Maggie was snoring as we drove and Matt's legs were stretched out in rest. Mike reached for my hand and squeezed it, and in the gesture I was reminded of church and kneeling and candles in hallowed halls right there in snores and legs and the smell of coffee. God gave us our hearts to love people, yes. And my heart was made to love the people in the car as I drove us all back home.

CHAPTER 9

Small Prayers

You pray in your distress and in your need;
would that you might pray also in the fullness
of your joy and in your days of abundance.
—KAHLIL GIBRAN, *THE PROPHET*

When we were dating, Mike gave me a piece of water-color art by Brian Andreas. He's an abstract artist who combines his colorful drawings with poetic mini stories, and I've always loved his work. I was only twenty or so when Mike gave it to me in his tiny garage apartment in the North End of Virginia Beach, and while I already knew he was the one for me, there was something about the gift that clarified it all: he knew me and understood me. Don't we all want to be known and understood and loved anyway? The poem now hangs in our hallway and is, in part, about saying the kind of small prayers that have always been so important to me, the ones I always said as a child. While starting to say these small prayers again as an adult was hard at first—I had to be very intentional about it—I now say them all day long. I'm a firm believer in observation being a form of prayer, and while I do pray more traditionally, too, I mostly just whisper prayers all day long. *Thank you, Lord, please don't let me forget this*, and *Dear God, please keep my children safe, healthy, and happy.*

When we were on vacation in Ocean City, Maryland, a few summers ago with my cousin and her family, we took a walk on Assateague Island. It was just my small family and my father. It was dusk and we walked to the end of a dock that stretched into the marshland of the bay. I walked with Maggie to the very edge and there she stood—one small girl looking out over the water. My father, husband, and son—men who have stolen my heart at various stages of my life—were right behind us, talking and laughing. I thought of how perfect a moment it really was and I silently said, *Thank you*, and closed my eyes very, very briefly and bowed my head, my daughter's hand tucked tightly and safely in my own. And almost as if in confirmation of my short prayer, I opened my eyes and saw that a dragonfly had landed on Maggie's finger. I've always loved dragonflies. Like my own eyes once were, her eyes were completely filled with awe, delight, joy. Her hair looked redder than blond in the setting sun, the last grandchild of a redheaded grandfather, my dad, who always wanted one of us to have his hair. None of us do, in the end. She beamed as the dragonfly stayed with her for a moment, long enough for us both to see it as a sign—grace personified, prayers answered. The dragonfly seemed to me to be a harbinger of goodness, reminding me that our small, hushed prayers matter.

One Sunday morning, before the sun was too high in the sky, I weeded our pumpkin patch as my children were in another part of the garden. I'm sure you all know what a pumpkin plant looks like, but just in case: it's not particularly special and some would say it's not even beautiful. It was just a pumpkin plant in the start of our first pumpkin patch. My husband and son were working in the enclosed garden and I was back behind the blueberry bush, weeding the start of the patch. Maggie was swinging nearby, but then they all took a walk to look at something or other and I was left alone with my task.

It was a lovely day as I remember—sunny and breezy— and it was suddenly quiet and I was alone. I had a strange moment in which I almost saw my hands from farther above, like I was looking down at my own hands working from afar. It was just perspective, I'm sure, but my hands seemed to be farther away than my arms could actually reach. I watched my hands work, seemingly as an outsider, and felt the breeze on my face. Weed by weed, I worked, and weed by weed, I prayed. This ordinary act of pulling weeds was a meaningful prayer for me.

When I picked the beautiful periwinkle hydrangea flowers from the plant that bloomed by the garage, I did the same. Many days, these are my prayers. Or I catch my husband looking at me from across the room or see a small white butterfly flutter in the brush and the noticing is the start. I hear my daughter say "I love you so much" to her brother and I pray a small *Thank you for the gift they have in one another—big brother and little sister.* Other times, the prayers are much more direct, pleas really, that don't seem small at all.

∞

In 2003 my own big brother, Ray, was in the Iraq War, and I was terrified I'd lose him, me the little sister who looks at him like my daughter looks at her own brother. I hadn't been to church in quite some time, but it was where I found myself again because I inherently knew, in the part of the soul that never forgets, that no one else could help him but God. I began attending church again, at the church down the road from our small apartment, the little place with the tiny porch on the third floor lofted up against the tree. It felt like a tree house, a reminder of home in the place that didn't quite feel like that yet.

That spring, the church had some sort of event going on—a scriptural comparison of *The Wizard of Oz*, I think. I don't remember any details, but I do remember the yellow brick road—it was also the road that led me back to the church, at least for a while. The pastor there was so very nice and welcoming, and there was an unexpected element to him I somehow found comforting. He smoked cigarettes after the service by the back door and while some might frown on that vice, I saw it as an expression of his humanity, the juxtaposition of the gray smoke from his mouth against his white collar of his ministry. I liked him; I liked how real he was. He accepted my journey, so I sat there on Sunday mornings with my flaws.

I begged God to allow Ray to make it home. I truly did. I *begged*. Maybe prayer isn't to be a begging; it's to be an offering, perhaps? But I have to say that in times of complete desperation like that one, I have pleaded, bartered, and begged. *Dear God, please,* please *bring my brother home and I promise to do better.* He did bring my brother home and for quite some time—years, really, over a decade and a half, actually—I've carried the weight of that guilt, the weight of a promise I didn't fulfill. But now I know God sees me—and you—as good enough. We don't need to beg or plead or barter and we don't need to make wagers or promises. We simply need to be grateful, even when that reminder comes in ways that don't seem divine at all. I came to that understanding over . . . mouse poop. Yes. Mouse poop.

Early one morning, fifteen years later, I randomly thought of Ray and texted him to see how he was. I think of him daily, but with children and lives unfurled and on separate coasts, we don't get to connect as much as I'd like. He texted back a photo of the place where Mary found out she was pregnant with Jesus. He was in Nazareth and while I knew he was going to Israel, I had forgotten the dates, so the photo took me off guard in the best possible way. I checked my text messages between classes, and there was the photo with a simple message: "This is where Mary found out she was pregnant with Jesus," and even in the picture, I saw and felt the holiness. For some reason, the image brought me to tears with its simple and rudimentary beauty—the image of her there, finding out her calling, her vocation, her high and holy purpose, above all others. And even though my brother wasn't in the photo, I pictured his image there, wondering if his eyes were ablaze. Even in the photo, I could feel the power of the place, the energy, the holiness.

I went about my day, teaching students, playing with my children and shuffling them to practices, doing my normal and rather ordinary things, but the photo stayed with me. Later, as I was wiping up the crumbs from the counters, I discovered the mouse poop. A country girl from an early age, I know what it looks like and have had plenty of experience with it. But I hadn't seen it since we'd moved into this house at the edge of the woods. I wasn't exactly surprised or even disgusted but instead marveled at my rather quiet acceptance of it. I breathed in the acknowledgment that we live by the woods, in a house near fields, knowing I had left too many crumbs on the counter, the debris of waffles still there from the rush of the morning.

I held it in my open palm and I stared at it, a tiny black

oblong piece of poop, debating my next move. If someone had been watching me, I'm sure I would have been
quite a sight. At almost the exact same time, my brother
sent me another photo from Mount Moriah, views of the
Mediterranean stretching like cirrus clouds, making it hard
to see if the sky was touching the sea. His dinner spot was
stunning, breathtaking, absolutely awesome. The makeshift
tables of pallets were set right on the mountaintop, right
where Abraham stood in the Bible, and they stretched across
the mountaintop with royal-blue pillows as seats, small nap-
kins and plates in front of each pillow on the pallet. I could
almost smell the food not pictured. I could see Ray standing
there, also not pictured. I could feel the air and smell what
I dream the Mediterranean smells like. I stared at the photo
on my phone in my right hand and back at the mouse poop
in my left. Back and forth my eyes darted, as I heard my
children arguing in the playroom and saw Frances chewing
a Superwoman doll. I didn't stop either.

It would be easy for me to wish I were in the photo—
with Ray, the steward from my youth. When I was little, I
looked to him the way an explorer uses a compass, and even
now, even as an almost forty-year-old woman, I still look
to him sometimes. Then my eyes darted to the poop in my
hand, but I did not wish I were there with him. I simply was
glad *he* was there, alive and well, breathing it in for us both.
I simply stood—and gave thanks for my brother, who was
in Israel and could send me the photo. *Thank you, Jesus, for
speaking, right here, right now, right in the middle of the*

mess, though I didn't say "mess." Yes, I swore in the prayer and I think God heard me. I know he did. The photo was holy enough. It was holy of holies—a confirmation that my brother does know me well, the sister who loves mountains and stories and to whom the best gift is a photo sent from halfway around the world. He teaches me even still, in ways he might not even know. The temple, Mount Moriah, and the gesture, coupled with the very realness of life—where he was in Israel and there in my kitchen in Pennsylvania—reached me where I was, and where I am is here, in the wilds of this life.

Here, the mornings are usually a cacophony—mostly the noises of all birds. I couldn't see the geese but I could hear them. I didn't get up from my place on the porch steps to find them; I was content with my hot cup of coffee. Mary, the cat, had greeted me at the door and hadn't left my side. That's kind of unusual for her, as she's the most independent of our cats, so I relished the chance to pet her. The sounds of the morning—the geese, the birds of every kind from the woods, our chickens, and the new ducks we got for the kids—combined with the rain falling, softly, almost as if it knew no one wanted it around that day, on the second day of summer break. There was something sweet on the air, some sort of flower—roses, maybe?—and I closed my eyes as the breeze blew, breathing in the smell. I pray like this on as many mornings as I can, small prayers fitted between my observations, longer prayers right before I come in the house to begin the day. Children often asleep in bed but the world so very awake, I gather my strength from the noises and the prayers and, of course, the coffee. Other days I pray as I braid hair.

＄

When I braided my daughter's hair for the first time, she sat very still on the bed in front of me, proud to have her hair braided like Mommy's, her curls straight enough from just getting out of the bath, the weight of the water pulling them down her back. Her hair is so different from mine— her light curls against my dark straight hair is always an image, a metaphor really, for she's the light to the darkness I carry. With her braid, our hair would be the same, if only for a time, united in the similar braids. She sat, fresh and scrubbed from the tub, smelling like lavender-vanilla goat soap and strawberry-ginger shampoo, me still with dirty hair and a face that wore the weight of the day, the weight of life, the circles under my eyes, so dark, the wrinkles getting deeper with each passing day. I once sat like she sat, my own mom's hands weaving my hair into a braid.

I sat, thankful—breathing in her goodness, her energy coming through my nose, helping me breathe. I gave thanks she was there, gifted from the other side to me. I prayed with each sweep of the hair, my fingers grazing her neck. She sat proud, her tiny back straight. The braid became my offering; it really did—the proof that I was grateful, the evidence that I was doing the work I was called to do.

Maggie turned and smiled, feeling her braid, long because her hair was still wet, but by the morning, it would shrink up and disappear into the curls that would fall from the weave of the braid. I hugged her, her tiny hands touching the braid that hung down my back. To her, it's me: it's the way she's come to see me—the mom with the dark hair and the braid, the mom she loves, despite all that I'm not.

She looked into my eyes and said, "Mommy, your eyes are green and mine are blue, but we both have long braids." I gathered her up in my arms again, my fingers finding her braid, my nose breathing in holy breaths, thankful breaths, breaths that made me think of holy beauty, everywhere, right there, right here, right then, right now, wet hair in my hands, braids falling down backs, life lived in small gestures, small braids, small hands. In deep breaths of lavender soap, of air, the kinds of breaths that will fill your soul if you'll let them. Holiness finds its way to us in snippets, in gasps, in breaths, in soap and hair and braids and hands and eyes and *in all of it.*

On the first day of school last year, as I was loading the kids up in the car, the fog rose from the mountains in front of our house, in small patches, drifting. I stopped and stared, and then my children did too. It was a beautiful image, one right in the middle of a harried morning, and I had a back-pack, a cup of coffee, and a jacket in my hands. We were

running a bit late, as usual. I told them we needed to stop
and watch the fog, if just for a moment, because stopping,
noticing, and paying attention to our lives right where we
are *is* prayer. We all stopped and did our noticing prayer
before I said, aloud, "Thank you, God, for this view." And
they said the same.

After school I began to wash the windows as the kids
rode their bikes in the driveway. I didn't get to all the panes,
but I made a valiant effort. After days and days of rain, the
sun was shining, and she was doing it magnificently, with
the most perfect breeze as the accompanist. We set to our
work—them, the important work of bike riding, and me, the
task of cleaning the very dirty windows. With each swipe
of my arm, I gave thanks for the boy and girl behind me,
wide-grinned, one with muck boots and the other with bare
feet, the sun dancing holy on their heads, halos calling. I
gave thanks for the house and this life I once only dared
to imagine. I prayed, *Please, dear God, don't let me* forget
*how amazing it is simply to be at my own home, with my
own small family.* This is a prayer we could use daily, simple
but powerful. It's so very powerful if we begin with *Please,
dear God, don't let me forget* _____ and then fill
in the blank. I pray daily always to remember Bermudan
blue–water eyes that remind me of our honeymoon, small-
hand goodbyes from the school steps, and hearty laughs of
my people. Small prayers. These small prayers help every
day, but especially on the hard days. They save me on the
harder days.

~

Sometimes, my exhaustion, like yours, I'm sure, can be palpable and fierce. And so, one day, months earlier, I simply sat and stared at the children playing in the yard in front of me. As my husband mowed the grass, I could smell the blades of green, fresh and musky, the promises of summer. Maggie pushed her baby bunny, Sugar, in a pink plastic shopping cart, and Matt ran with Frances. And I sat, my shoulders slumped, my head up but my eyes down, staring at my feet in flip-flops. It wasn't at all time for them yet with winter still hanging on, but still I wore them. I stared at my feet and quietly said the prayers I pray all day long, *Dear God, please protect my children. Please send your angels to watch over them and to keep them safely tucked in their wings.* I looked up moments later when the mower stopped, my husband jumping off to the greeting of the dog and then the kids, just like they had hours before when he'd pulled up the driveway—the flood of his brood, two human children and one canine.

When he had come home from work earlier, Matt, Maggie, and Frances all ran to his Jeep at record speeds, anxious in their own ways to make him their own, the dog jumping on his chest for a hug, Matt going on and on about something that happened at school, Maggie asking him to push her on the swing. *Thank you for the constant who is my husband*, I prayed when I saw him. I was an observer first when he got out of the Jeep and then again later, when they rushed to the mower to him. And I stood up and walked toward them, tired, yes, but it was time for us to go inside and get ready for bed. Then they rushed to make *me* their own, nestling beside me and asking me to tell them a story or sing "Blackbird" by the Beatles. I was renewed. *Thank you.*

I generally type as the day ends, the clicking of the keys as my fingers hit them, my eyes looking up and out the windows in front of me, the cats both asleep on my car, another cat—not ours—in the driveway. This cat has been hanging around, eating and resting here. Our cats don't seem alarmed or upset, and we all simply watch the new cat and try to befriend it.

She's gray against the green of the grass, different from the calicos who are usually resting on my car, as she makes her approach for her nighttime meal. I tap, tap, tap, willing my fingers to do the work I know I must do to get my word count in, when Maggie comes and crawls in my lap and I pause, never too busy—*Lord, please don't ever allow me to be too busy*—to stop and hold her, to sing to her, to look right into her face smudged with chocolate. My children are used to this routine—my writing a bit while they eat a snack and then while they jump in showers or tubs and get ready for bed. It's the routine we're in: I sit at the window and write and they eat in the living room behind me and bathe and shower in the bathroom to my left. I'm here—right in the middle of the evening as it ends, for them, for me, for the cats. The tapping, the eating, the bathing, the sun as it sets; even on this cloudy day, I can see it. The clouds have made wispy shapes over the field in sharp contrast to the mountains, always changing colors, navy blue in that light. It's the ending of the day, the ritual of the evening, the holding and tucking in.

Later, as they drift to sleep, I pray about them and for them. And while all of this is a daily occurrence, I try not to take it for granted. I falter sometimes, but I'm learning and, in the end, that's not a failure at all. I stop and remember these are my holy offerings, the small prayers said in hushed voices. *Thank you, thank you, thank you.* Often, it's the only prayers I say in a day. Whispered prayers, even (and especially?) small ones in the midst of the mundane, make a difference in our perception of our lives. The silent prayers, the *murmured in the hush of the morning* prayers, the rush of the day prayers, or the quiet of the evening prayers—these small prayers truly help us to see this life, this one *right here*, as holy—everywhere, holy.

CHAPTER 10

And the Rain Falls

For after all, the best thing one can do
When it is raining, is to let it rain.

—HENRY WADSWORTH LONGFELLOW

It was pouring down rain here a few nights ago, with cold rain falling on our metal roof, making a sound I've come to love. My husband said to me, "I always wanted a metal roof," and I agreed. The rainfall gives the house a different kind of peace; the rain has a sound as it hits the roof, making it seem even that more real. When I was a little girl, our house had a big front porch—the kind with a swing on the end. My dad's favorite thing to do, or one of his favorite things, was and is to sit on the porch and listen to the rain or to watch a storm roll in, announcing the rain sure to follow. I loved it, too, but I also remember sitting on the porch as a child and venturing down the steps simply to stand in the rain, my arms raised to my sides, rain on my open palms, landing in drips on my fingertips. Like my dad, the porch is also one of my favorite places—on my own big front porch in a rainstorm. I wonder if I've loved the rain because I've thought of it as water falling from the sky—nature's way to show us how to let go—but even more than that, the water as holy and cleansing as it is unleashed from the skies above.

The first winter we had Frances, I took her outside to go to the bathroom and it was snowing—big, beautiful flakes, the kind of snow that looks as if it's orchestrated by some sort of symphony we can't hear, the flakes falling like notes do. It fell in beautiful sheets and I simply stood and let it fall on me. As Frances danced around, still very much a puppy and in the first snow she'd seen, I stood and listened to the snow as it fell. Snow seems to have its own sound and I can actually hear it if I listen closely enough. I listened. I looked up. And the snow fell softly on my cheeks. That morning, I was stumbling under the pressure of a full day and the snow felt like it was falling as a daily baptism by water of sorts, a way I could meet God before the rush of the day. As it hit my cheeks, it melted and I stood and let it wet them before being brought back to my dog, right at my feet, covered in snow, my face wet.

What can be holier than the water falling right from God's hands onto our heads? I love that image—him commanding the snow and rain to fall, both being sent to wash us clean, day after day. Holy water, free for the taking, fresh from the sky, but falling all the same. Rain and snow as a chance to begin again, to grow, to change, to drown the parts of us we no longer need. I didn't always feel this way, really, as I struggled for years with the idea of baptism, the formal traditions I'd grown up with that I wasn't quite sure mattered and my place in them.

But when my daughter was baptized in the small stone church, she jumped toward the small marble font of water in one very surprising lunge and, suddenly, I was sure. My husband had a good hold on her but she surprised him. There's a photo of the moment and even the pastor was surprised, a smile on her own face. The photo of us in that moment is pure joy and *all is well*. It was like Maggie knew the power of the water, and she's loved the water since. A girl never too afraid to take off her shoes and socks and wade in the river with her older brother and cousins, she knows the way water can heal and she's reminded me of it. She's laughed as the rain has fallen onto her curls and she's reminded me that I can laugh at what might have once seemed like a misfortune to me—rain soaking my hair—but now is welcomed. Maggie is a lover of all things water—a lover of baths, the ocean, or the bay we visit every summer with my cousin and her family; I think she's come to know the Spirit moves in these places. And because of her, I know it too. She loves Vance Joy's song "Fire and the Flood," and just this morning, when it came on the radio, she said to me, "Mama, remember this song! I love this song! You used to sing it to me when I was a little baby." Yes, she knows the power of water but she's the fire in my life, in the flood of life she rode when she was born. She's a holy flame set against the holy water of it all.

GO

When I studied abroad in England, I became more familiar with the rain than I ever had before. I know it's a cliché, perhaps, to talk about the rain in England, but it's true: it rains a lot. I got used to it and learned to love the rainy days. I charged my new accommodations on a credit card I had taken out on the college campus I went to in Pennsylvania and my room wasn't the greatest. I slept on a mattress in the corner of the room and right above it, in the ceiling, was a window—the kind that just opens with no screen. It was a tilt window right above my head and I loved to have it open. A nature lover living in the middle of a city for the first time in my life, the open window made me feel more connected to nature and home.

On some nights, I'd lie there and stare at the stars, but on most nights it was cloudy. On some occasions, I wouldn't tilt the window at the right angle to prevent the rain from coming in. An American not at all used to British norms, I'd often wake up to the rain dripping on my face. Oddly, I came to welcome it. That might sound strange because, in many ways, we've come to think of rain as the ultimate destroyer of plans—the ruin of picnics, vacations, games. But I've come to see rain as holy, as nourishing, and as a central Pennsylvanian who grew up around so many farms, I know well that rain means sustenance and growth. In England, it became kind of a metaphor for me as my own symbol of growth. I grew so very much from those rainy days, as the rain seemed to grow me.

In the rain of England, I met a kindred spirit, the kind of friend most of us only meet once in a lifetime, the kind I've been lucky enough to have a few times over, the kind Anne talks about in *Anne of Green Gables*. Together, on the weekends, we traveled around on very tight budgets. We packed peanut butter and jelly sandwiches and ate multigrain fruit bars, and because of my own financial constraints, we walked in the rain often instead of taking the bus. She did that for me and taught me that friends simply *walk with you*, often with no questions asked. They walk in the rain because you can't afford the bus.

In Wales, we hiked a waterfall in pouring rain, and we didn't stop until we reached the top. I remember looking at her, her blond hair drenched, and she looked at me, completely soaked in a coat that wasn't waterproof, and we smiled as the water fell from the falls and from the sky. The sound was something I'll never forget—the gushing, the falling, the water reminding us that it's okay to fall, to falter, to give in. I vividly remember the moment as holy even though, at the time, I wasn't sure how such a thing even could be. I know *now* how well it can be.

It's moments like these—the listening to water, the falling of it on our faces, the giggling of children as they wade in the river, the ducks dipping their heads into the stream—that we can remember the redeeming power of the daily water we encounter.

But there's another lesson, almost as powerful—the power of letting go. This one returns over and over again for me. I need to learn to unclench my hands, but I have already learned something that helps me: the beauty of the letting go of another sort—the literal fall, the descent, the rain coming from the sky, the rising and falling of the tides, the flow of the rivers. Waterfalls, like the one in Wales, or the mountain streams so familiar here in Pennsylvania, flowing over rocks and falling, downward, show us the beauty of the fall. The rivers flow in one direction and with one mission: to reach the ocean. The tide consistently rises and falls, the waves lapping on and receding from the shore. It's a beautiful image, if we're paying attention, right in front of us as we sit on a busy beach. The bay laps so rhythmically, the kind of steady rocking I've come to love, sitting on the end of the dock, the kind that my cousin says "sets her straight" when she needs it. All of the water's actions seem to help us learn how to adjust to the rising and falling in our own lives.

When the acorns first start to fall on our metal roof every fall season, I jump. Because of my struggles with anxiety, I know the fear of falling that is downright terrifying—the kind that leaves you clinging, nails dug in, tears streaming down your face. But I look back on those times, and I hope you will, too, knowing that you will rise stronger, braver, more or less sure, depending on what you need to learn. Isn't it interesting how some of us need to be *less* sure? We don't *need* to know everything. We don't need to be so sure. Sometimes, not being sure is what will move us beyond the place we're in. It's the relying and the being terrified that push us to stand up again, in faith alone.

Most of us have learned how to tread water and keep our heads above the waves that reach to the shore and back to the ocean. Maybe the water that looks likely to gobble us up really just wants to reach the ocean. Or maybe the looming wave that looks as if it's trying to pull you under is actually trying *to help you* reach the shore, the shore you were called to see, the one you know is there but you just cannot reach on your own. It might seem like it wants to pull you under, and it will if you don't float, tread, or doggy paddle. But the wave means only to move you, to carry you beyond to a place you wouldn't go otherwise.

My mom tells me I loved the water when I was a child. Her father, my Pop-Pop, also loved the water and I loved everything he did. My mom, a strong swimmer, wanted all of us to be good swimmers too. My parents had a small above-ground pool in the backyard of our house in a blue-collar neighborhood outside of Philadelphia before we moved to central Pennsylvania. My mom always has said, "You knew how to swim before you could walk." I'm not sure if that's really true or just an exaggeration, but I love the image of a little Kara, not scared of water, not scared of the fall—a Kara *not afraid*. When I need to be less afraid, I picture that Kara, ready to jump.

I was just a little girl—maybe around eight or so—when my long-legged brother, a good swimmer and around thirteen years old, tackled the churning ocean waves one summer. Fearless, he was confident of his abilities, but a huge wave pulled him under with its undertow. I don't remember many details, except my mother's fear, the waves with their whitecaps, and his emerging safely. Honestly, since then, I've just watched the ocean, in awe of its power but not so sure of my own. It's kind of how I watched the world, *the fear looming*, sure of *its* power but not so sure of my own.

∞

Many years later, when I was a senior in high school, I felt very alone—sad because Mike was away in the navy and one of my best friends had graduated. Looking back and being more aware now of who I am, I realize I was depressed. I had never stopped missing my brother—he'd been away for years—and I desperately missed my old house, only fifteen minutes away from the new one. The one light in an otherwise dismal year was Daisy.

During military training, my brother left behind his golden retriever, Daisy, because she wasn't allowed on base during the training, of course. She stayed with us for six months, and in those six months, my dream of having a dog to wake me in the morning came true. My mom would tell her, "Go wake up Kara," and Daisy would run up the steps, jump on my bed, and lick my face. Every morning started that way during that half year and I came to see her as a best friend. She was the substitute for everything and everyone I missed. I loved Daisy. We had left my childhood home right before my senior year and it was Daisy who helped me see the beauty in living where we had moved. Our new-to-us house was right on the Juniata River and Daisy loved it. I didn't care much for the water, but Daisy showed me its rewards.

At the end of the street my parents live on now, past the last house, there is a trail through the woods by the river. If you walk down it far enough, you'll come to the most beautiful part of the river, where the river widens and the sun shines freely, free from trees hanging far into the center. In the middle of the river, there's a huge rock. Back then, I'd wade out—the river never deeper than my knees at that point—with a book in my hand, always my go-to reprieve from the real life that made me sad. Daisy would swim out. Together, we'd settle on the rock. I'd read and she'd rest in the sun, and I remember feeling happy and being surprised. Growing up by a very small stream—what central Pennsylvanians call a crick instead of creek—it wasn't until this river experience that I fell in love with the water. It always felt kind of like cheating on my childhood home if I came to like anything about this new one, and there was plenty to like: the river, the 1920s Craftsman with its interesting nooks, the shorter commute to school, the proximity to McDonald's (I've always loved french fries!). I was close to my high school and to my after-school job, and life without the longer commute from our rural home seemed easier. But it was Daisy who brought me to the river, who taught me to embrace the water in all the metaphorical ways.

When Ray finished his training and took her back with him, my heart broke. I cried and vividly remember him saying, "Kara, you can keep her," and he meant it, but I knew how much he loved her and needed her. I let her go and off they went. I never quite got over losing her. Fourteen years later, at a ripe old age, Daisy died in my brother's home in California. Both of us married with babies, I cried over the phone when he told me. I loved Daisy maybe more than I had ever loved any animal, even my own old golden, still alive at the time but ailing, having overcome her own surgery for a cancerous tumor. The pain of losing Daisy was real, even though she wasn't my dog. She'd never really been mine to have, but she felt more mine than most anything ever had.

Months later, Ray brought her ashes back and, with his wife, spread Daisy in that river, upstream from where she and I used to wade, swim, and read. And I never said this to anyone then, but it was like a full circle for me, a passage and chapter closed, a reminder that we can love more than one thing, one dog, one place. Daisy taught me that, actually, for she loved my brother first but quickly and fiercely loved me, the way only a dog can. And that river is sacred to me now, partially because she's in it.

The Susquehanna River is that way now for my husband, as I found out one Sunday on the way to New York City. It was just Mike, Matt, and me, as Maggie stayed behind with my parents. As we drove through a very beautiful part of Pennsylvania, the northern landscape of the Pocono Mountains, I was enchanted with the fog rising from the mountains, as I usually am, for the fog lifting seemed like God whispering his promises to all of us. I watched it rise, imagining murmurs of grace and goodness, handouts of all that is good and holy in the world, straight from his hand. It was a Sunday and watching the mist rise from the mountains felt sacred enough to me. *Sacred Sunday at its best*, I thought, as I often do.

I watched the mist rise from the mountains from my window, in a trance, completely under the spell of the mist rising, smokelike and billowing. I love fog over a mountain. It's my most favorite view. When we crossed the Susquehanna, I turned to tell Matt in the back seat, only to glance left at Mike. I was surprised to see him make the sign of the cross and when I asked him why, he told me it was because of his cousin, who drowned in the very same river, hundreds of miles from here but the same river all the same. *Water to water*, just like *ashes to ashes*, I thought.

I didn't know he did that. What could be more prayerful, more sacred, than the remembering of those who returned to ash, to water?

I now know that we can crave places and I often dream of the river, the way it wraps and flows under the iron bridge near my hometown, the way it laps a little in one spot near my parents' house, the way it foams there by the shore. As I finish this chapter, it is sunny and I'm watching the ferns move outside my window, the irises so purple suddenly out there and in the vase of flowers I try to keep next to my computer. I have a collection of flowers from my mom, a bouquet of pale pink peonies, white ones, too, and purple irises—my favorites—in a turquoise vase. She knows my love of flowers; I inherited it from her. Every 250 words typed, I allow myself a sniff of a peony. And even as they are beautiful and so is my view of the gold of the field outside my window, all I can see is that river and where the sun dances on it in spots, the light hitting it in the most spectacular light show. I'd have a hat on and sunglasses, my white legs bare to get some sun. My mind is there today. My mind is on the water.

The water and the dream of it come to me from time to time, and for me, it's a reminder to take the time I need to find the water, to remember grace, to begin again, to welcome the descent, to let go. I stand in the falling rain when I can and almost never have an umbrella. We always dry, after all. My dad is a poet and wrote this beautiful poem about rain. He sent it to me in a text once, a gift of words because he knows my favorite gifts. The poem is titled "Rain":

> Rain, rain, come and stay
> Wash away the noise of yesterday
> Take a moment to look around
> And to recall our feet on earth's sun-parched
>   ground
> Let us remember your gentle and calming sound
> And help us never to forget
> That because of you, life abounds.
>
> —RAYMOND LAWLER SR. (MY DAD), 2017[1]

Rain, come and stay. Let's not try to stop it. Let's try not to wipe it away or curse its name. Please, let it *wash it all away*. Help us remember that the water, the rain, the lapping ocean, the almost drowning, the learning to doggy paddle, *all of it*, is to help us grow and reach the shore. Let us not try to stop the rain.

❧

I thought I was done with this chapter, but it's raining today on the day I'm editing it; it's been raining for days. For days, buckets have dropped from the skies, unleashing so much water. It's not just a sprinkle or a rain shower. This is a rain that floods, sweeps away everything, turns part of the yard into a pond; Jemima and Delila, our ducks, swim in it. I love those ducks. They're beautiful when you really look at them. Mike knows it and pulled me to the window, pointed, and said, "Look how the rain beads up on their backs." Jemima, a Pekin, is white and large, right out of the Beatrix Potter tales I loved so much as a child. Delila is a mallard, female, with brown feathers, small blocks of turquoise on the back ones.

The rain falls fast and I could lament. Maggie and I met our friends, a mother and a daughter, at Barnes & Noble. Maggie, at four, has friends now. The little girls, with their similar blond curls, played at the train table and ate matching blondie bars. My friend and I sat and talked about life and then I felt life. She grabbed my hand and put it on her belly and her baby moved—an elbow bent or a knee maybe. I smiled, wanting to keep my hand there, remembering. The baby is due in one month; in one month the water will come and the baby will breathe and cry out life, grace right from the Maker. It rains today and I could lament, but we all know we need water for life, the wading in it necessary, the hands getting wet and catching, the baby crying. It's raining and I can't stop the rain, but I wouldn't anymore. Not now.

We came home after seeing our friends and the road had flooded, orange, triangular Road Closed signs blocking our path. Muddy brown water from the river was over the road and I turned the car around. I drove home another way, for there is always another way, I'm learning, to the warm house on the hill. All afternoon the four of us have lounged, books and blankets, iPads and football games, the warmth of candles and coffee and socked feet brushing one another's. And the rain falls. And we live our life not despite it but *with* it, all rose and bergamot candle, warm baths a rain's comfort, cotton towels meeting bodies, all toasty. And while the rain falls, we live our life and say our thanks for it. Holy rain falls from the sky. Holy abundance abounds. *Help us never to forget*, like my dad wrote in his poem. Holy *is* everywhere, and often in the things that surprise us, like the falling rain on what should be a sunny day.

CHAPTER 11

Angels on Guard

He ordered his angels to guard
you wherever you go.

—PSALM 91:11

Every year, I read Samuel Coleridge's "Rime of the Ancient Mariner" with my twelfth-grade English students, and it opens with a Latin quote from theologian Thomas Burnet about there being "more visible than invisible natures."[1] I've always sat with that line in the years since I first read it in Manchester, England, while going to school. But it really hasn't been until the most recent years that I've made sense of these lines written almost four hundred years ago. Believing in God is believing in someone we've never seen, but we can absolutely see the work of him and his angels all around us, and often.

It was late in May. The sun was setting but it wasn't dark. Still, it was almost eight thirty on a school night right before the end of the school year, and I pulled Matt's curtains shut to block out the reminder that there was still day left, still time to play according to the rhythm of the earth, not the schedules we all keep. He was tired with a hint of sun under his eyes where the sunscreen missed. On this particular night, in a rare turn of events, he decided I didn't need to lay down with him like I usually do and that he could fall asleep on his own. He said, "You know, Mom, I'll snuggle up down here and say the guardian angel prayer and then I'll go to sleep because I know the angel is watching over me."

The picturing of angels on guard is something I've done since I was a little girl, small and sure that an angel followed me. It was talked about in our house, and I had a picture in my room of two small children walking across a precarious bridge, an angel's wings surrounding them and ushering them over the broken bridge, keeping them safe from the raging waters below. I used to stare at the picture, sure of my own angel and imagining all the times I was protected.

When we first moved here to this house on the hill, we didn't know what four of our trees were, nor did I know the significance of the trees to my dad. One night he was here and, together with Mike, discovered that the trees are, in fact, chestnut trees. I've come to learn from Dad that chestnut trees aren't as plentiful as they once were, and he was very excited to see them here at our house.

As we examined the nuts, not yet ready for harvest, he told me how much his father, my Pop-Pop Buddha, loved chestnuts. I never knew him so I drink in every detail I can learn about him and what he was like—what made him smile and what he liked to eat or do or drink or see. No detail goes unappreciated. And through stories about him over the past forty years, I have come to know him, even though we've never met. I love people I've never even really known and I can tell you it's possible.

Now I know Buddha loves chestnuts and so I will love them too. My dad told stories of roasting chestnuts over an open fire, and here at this house, I can see my Pop-Pop Buddha walking out in front of our house, gathering chestnuts in the small orchard with my children, whom I know he would have loved. I can see him here, clear as day, roasting chestnuts in the open fire in the fireplace in our kitchen. And as I picture him here, I have this feeling that he's watching us and keeping us all safe, one of the angels in our midst. The image often sustains me.

GD

One April, I had the busiest week of the year ahead of me and my body could feel it—the weight as I swung my legs over the side of the bed extra early, searching for my pink leather slippers that weren't there, as usual. I leave them all over the house. Where had I left them this time? Cold feet begged for them and in that one moment, the day began— the hustle of the day, the waking of the kids, the packing of lunches, the making of breakfast, the commute to schools. The shuffle was on; the chaos had begun, with a schedule for the week way too packed for my comfort. I still hadn't written answers to questions for an interview that day about my writing, and I got up early to make quiche for a teacher appreciation breakfast at the kids' school. I had a long and daunting week ahead—filled with blessings, *yes, yes, yes*, but just so busy with things every night of the week— practices, volunteer things, life. Plus, I was up, worried, with a toothache for much of the night. I hate going to the dentist—absolutely disdain it—and I apologize to anyone in the dental profession for that. My mom used to tell me not to use the word *hate*, but it's fitting here. My dental anxiety is extreme, and while I do go to the dentist, I do it after much procrastination and dread for weeks before the said appointment. It's not pretty.

So imagine my distress when I woke up in the middle of the night with a bad toothache. I suspected the worst and catastrophized: I'd have to go to the dentist without prior warning, planning, or excessive worrying. I expected the worst: extraction or a root canal. After I dropped the kids off at school, I drove to a local doughnut shop drive-through for a coffee. I sat in line, waiting to order my favorite: an Americano, black. It's mostly all I drink anymore, and as I've said before, I think coffee can cure most any woe. I had the window slightly rolled down to enjoy the crisp air of the morning, and I sat behind a black Ford F-150, discouraged, head down, heart heavy. I prayed, *Dear God, how will I do this? Not just the dentist appointment, I mean, but all of it?* I closed my eyes as I said the words, just for a few seconds, my head on the steering wheel. The wind blew and I opened my eyes to see a palm at my steering wheel. This might sound unbelievable, but it happened.

It was a Palm Sunday palm, the kind they pass out in church to celebrate the beginning of Holy Week, the day Jesus rode into Jerusalem. It was beat up, browned, and weathered. Somehow, it blew into my window—a full palm in the drive-through of a doughnut shop, amid car exhaust and noise and the smell of doughnuts—but it almost seemed to have been placed. I held it in my hands, my hands shaking from stress, the palm brittle and brown, and my eyes welled with tears. Many will say it was just a strange coincidence, but I am sure the palm was a message to me that day, a message to continue on the journey, a sign that God was with me. In the mess of what was my car—remnants of toys and snacks scattered about—I had a holy moment, right there in what my husband calls my "clumpster" (half closet, half dumpster). It was truly one of the holiest moments of my life, the verification for me of my guardian angel, of all being *enough* and well. There are angels by our sides and I truly think one was outside my car that very day, but I also have felt their presence in other ways.

Each morning, when I drive the kids to school, I pass two people—the police officer on the corner watching to ensure the children get to school safely, patrolling for anything amiss. And I pass a crossing guard doing the same, in her own way. Both of them are white-haired, and I often wonder if they know one another, streets away, patrolling different corners, ushering children. They make me feel safe as I drop my children off at the school, silent prayers on my lips as I watch Matt turn and walk away from me up the stairs and into doors, blowing a kiss to me at the top of the steps before heading into his classroom. I walk Maggie in and turn her over to her teacher. I pray for them, *Dear God, please keep my children safe today. Send your angels to wrap their wings around them and all the children, ushering them through their days.* Small prayers are on my lips as I drive away, but they carry the weight of my entire world, really. And there's always a weight of sadness as the kids turn away from me, not extreme, not too much to bear anymore but there every day, and then I turn the corner and see the crossing guard with her white hair and her black hat and I wave at her as I come to a full stop at the stop sign. She always waves back and, in that gesture, there's always a feeling of *all is well, Kara. All is well.* These people, whom I've never met and never spoken to, have become a part of each morning. I look for them and, so far, in three years' worth of mornings, they've been standing on their corners, ushering children, keeping a watchful eye. And then I wonder, almost every day, if they're the angels I've prayed for God to send. Could it be that simple? Could they be right there? Just maybe? Maybe this is how you find holiness? I think so. It can show up in ways we don't expect; of this I am sure.

⌒

Just as Daisy woke me up years ago, Frances has a similar habit. Each morning, she jumps on Matt's bed, waking him, and with that movement, I say, "Super Dog!" She pounces on the bed after impatiently waiting on the steps like an excited child, the baby gate in the way of *her* children, *her* kids, the ones asleep in the beds upstairs. She knows I won't let her wake them too early, and so it's a waiting game, a waiting game of her looking at me and then back up the steps where my babies are nestled and dreaming. Frannie and I are up before the sun comes up most mornings, Mike before me with her. I relieve him when he goes to work because she can't be trusted up, awake, and alone. She's still too much of a puppy.

We woke Matt one morning, as usual, and after saying "Aw, hi, Frannie," he looked at me, still with sleep in his eyes, the haze of a dream on his mind, and told me about a dream he had that early morning. Frances woke him right from his dream where he was fighting a dragon with Maggie by his side. They were winning, only because there was an angel there too. I loved the imagery and told him so, and we smiled at the thought of the angel. Always the interpreter of symbols, I search for them often in my day-to-day life. Later, I thought about the symbolism I saw in his dream. Saint Michael the Archangel is the leader of God's army in the fight against the Devil, who is often depicted as a dragon. The image sat with me, strengthened me, and reminded me that there really is an army of angels at my back, and I know they're with my kids too. But I get reminders on the regular.

One afternoon, Maggie was showing me how well she could ride on her balance bike. Round and round the driveway she went, singing, "Grooving and cruising!" I urged her on and truly was amazed at how quickly she'd picked it up— the riding of a balance bike without pedals, her bare feet up in the air, smiling as she went around in circles. I cheered, "Go, Maggie," just before she took a turn too quickly and fell onto the asphalt of the driveway. She cried instantly, that sort of silent cry that is scary. I ran to her and while she seemed fine, big tears rolled down her hot, red cheeks. I scooped her up and she hid her face in my shoulder, her back heaving with sobs.

It was then when I saw a small white butterfly. I'm no stranger to butterflies appearing near Maggie; they do often. Since she's been little, they've flown around her. It seems that I've seen more butterflies since she was born than I did in my lifetime before her. I told her to watch the butterfly and she did. It flew all around her head and her sobs slowed down until she stopped crying completely. I know this might be hard to believe and, quite honestly, it does seem coincidental, but the butterfly flew away as soon as Maggie stopped crying. We watched it flutter off before I said, "Maggie, I think that's your guardian angel, always near you." She looked at me and smiled before she jumped out of my arms and back onto her bike, her song loud again in the mountain air of the summer morning. The butterfly was gone, but not the message that she's looked after, cared for, and always encircled with wings, in one way or another.

My Pop-Pop passed away when I was almost three, and for days, I told my mom he was there, playing with me and visiting me, like he normally did in life. I don't remember this—the line between him being alive and his death—but she tells me I didn't understand it at all, but I didn't question it either. I was so certain and sure and she always wondered if I never questioned his presence because I was too little to understand his death. Often, even now, I ask my mom to tell me the story simply because I love hearing the tale being told. And there is a very big part of me that knows—like deep down in the part of my soul that never forgets—he was there, visiting me from the other side. My mom thinks so, too, and he reminds me of his presence from time to time, even still.

One night when Maggie was around two, she took a spot next to Matt on her bed for her nightly bedtime story.

On her bedside table, there is a photo of my Pop-Pop. Even though my grandfathers and one of my grandmothers have passed away, along with both of Mike's grandfathers and one of his grandmothers, we try to keep them a part of our lives with photos and objects around the house. We even have a beautiful painting of Mike's grandfather, done by Mike's cousin, hanging large in our living room, and Maggie loves to drink from my grandmother's yellow teacup. Even though our children have never met our grandparents who have passed away, it's important to us for them to be reminded of them and feel protected by them. Matt reads to Maggie most every night, but out of the blue, that night, she looked at the photo and said, "Pop-Pop, do you like this story?" I smiled and Matt said, "Mom, maybe he is here, listening." When I tucked Maggie in after the story, she took her time kissing her babies before she turned to the photo of Pop-Pop and said, "Pop-Pop, I'll see you tomorrow." Just like that, final and matter-of-fact. She'd never done that before. She crawled under her covers certain of me and the moon shining brightly outside her window and the fact that Pop-Pop would visit her tomorrow. She has no uncertainty in her personality; she's always sure, and this was no exception.

When Maggie said my Pop-Pop would be around the following day, it was like that part of my soul was jolted. *How could she know?* Maybe she didn't, but I like to think that just maybe he visits us, an angel in our midst here on the hill from time to time, walking with Buddha. I picture them talking with one another as they walk through the front yard and swing on our porch swings, sipping coffee. They smile at my children as they play on the porch and run in the yard. They bend down and softly kiss the tops of their heads right before the sun sets. Maybe Pop-Pop was visiting us that night, just like Matt said. I think picturing angels on guard helps us to find holy wherever we are, no matter our circumstances.

When anxiety had gotten the best of me, I scheduled a very rare massage to help me relax. When I first arrived, the massage therapist told me to tell her when I was under the blankets and ready for her to come into the massage room. There were candles in the room and soft light, and the warm blankets immediately made me feel safe. She came in and set to work on my neck, tight with anxiety.

For years, I've been told, in subtle and indirect ways, from various people, to deal with the issues that cause my back to seize, but I never listened until I had no other option, when there was no way back up other than to climb out. And in the middle of climbing out I was thinking of that image—me climbing up a ladder, up and out of a hole— when she was rubbing a knot from my neck. For about an hour, she massaged the tension from my body and momentarily I forgot most of my worries. When she said I was very peaceful, that the core of me was not shaken and that my trial was almost ending, I looked up at her, surprised. She repeated that my core wasn't shaken and said something about there being a lot of activity around me. I didn't ask what she meant, but instead I pictured an aura all around me and put my head back in the headrest, as she laid her hands on my head, in silence I've always supposed was prayer. And even if it wasn't, that day, it was all of that to me—hands praying over my head, the confirmation that my battle was ending and angels were with me. The image of them, at my head, wings of glory, carried me from that room and back into the life that had been waiting for me, a confirmation of everywhere holy, and angels all around, on guard.

CHAPTER 12

The World Within

"I do not ask for any crown,
   But that which all may win;
Nor seek to conquer any world
   Except the one within."

—LOUISA MAY ALCOTT, *UNDER THE LILACS*

I love you and Daddy and Matt and myself," Maggie said. I smiled, noticing the last person she added in the list, and said, "That's so good to love yourself, Maggie." She replied, "It's because God says we should love yourself and your

friends and family." Those were her exact words, a little girl
about to turn four. I assumed she'd heard it at school and
I spent time that day thinking about it. How often do we
act like we love ourselves? When we list the people we love,
do we ever think about adding ourselves to the list? I never
have. Mostly we chronicle how we don't love ourselves—
our "too-big" calves that actually are so very strong and
mean that we can walk and walk for miles on end without
growing weary or our anxious nature, with our tendency to
overthink or worry instead of perhaps turning things over
to God. Some of us even pick apart every minute detail of
ourselves, and many women struggle at some point in their
lifetimes to love themselves as they are. I sure have. I sure
do. I've fallen into the trap of believing that I'm "too" this or
"too" that, not enough of this or that. This has manifested
with issues with weight and body image, but also with self-
acceptance, in general, and this has been my hardest chapter
to write *because I'm right here, in it*. But I think one of the
most important parts of seeing holiness everywhere is to see
it in ourselves—to conquer the world within—as hard as
that might be.

I once was told I was my own worst enemy. The words
came after a disagreement, and I allowed myself to be
destroyed by them. I was destroyed because I didn't disagree
with them and in fact, I *agreed*, and it was like a confirmation to me of all my flaws. I'm an overthinker and someone
who tends to analyze most every situation. It's not always
pretty, unfortunately, and I've mostly disliked that about

myself. Underneath a confident exterior, my true nature always lingered: I'm sensitive, I overthink, and I worry when I wish I wouldn't.

Being told by someone I cared about, though, that I was my own worst enemy made my knees buckle because it was the ultimate judgment for me, the ultimate *you are not worthy* statement. And while that part *wasn't* written and maybe not even meant in the end, it's how I felt about myself. I fought back tears walking through the grocery store, over the picking out of red peppers, the ones Maggie likes so much, and my mind raced all day. *I am my own worst enemy. Why would anyone like me? I should stop writing. What could I possibly teach people about finding holiness or identity or beauty, as flawed as I am? Maybe I'm a fraud. I'm far from an example. I can't follow this call of writing, Lord; please don't make me. I'm too broken.* The negative self-talk was almost too much to bear, but familiar all the same.

I remembered back to all the times I've made steps forward with perfectionism, body acceptance, showing grace, overreacting, or even with my issues with anxiety, only to be knocked down by my own actions, the only actions we can control, after all. When I was told I was my own worst enemy, I believed it was *true*. I was afraid that my words in this book would resonate with no one. I'd be found to be an imposter. At the heart of it all was this: Do I believe in myself? Do I like myself? Do I even accept those things myself? *Who am I anymore, anyway?*

My tendency to overthink and analyze, coming to conclusions—some accurate and some not—has been both a blessing and a curse, and on many days it's actually *felt* like a curse. But after so much self-reflection I've realized, in some ways, it is my gift. Could it be both? My worst enemy and my greatest gift? Sometimes what holds us back can also propel us forward. If I didn't have the ability to read faces and situations, analyze word choice and tone, and look at the way sentences are strung together, like beads on a necklace—the true purposefulness that goes into it all—I'd never be an English teacher. I get paid to dissect words and tone; I get paid to illuminate meaning and interpret symbol. I also wouldn't be much of a writer if I couldn't do those things. Most writers I know churn words the way Mike likes to churn homemade ice cream, and it's pretty hard to turn off, even as I try. And I do try, but I can hardly read anymore without analyzing, and while I try hard not to apply this to all words, sometimes, I fall short. Even in (and *especially* in) my own words, I fall even shorter. I constantly overthink my own words and reactions and am often critical of them.

But my "enemy" of overthinking and overanalyzing has led me to two callings: teaching and writing. It has given me the ability to look into people's faces and relate to them, even if I sometimes misread intentions or emotions. It's exactly why I notice the fog rising from the mountain, the peace on a newborn's face, or the joyful twinkle of my daughter's eyes as she dances in the driveway. Yes, I overthink, and it's led me into some dark, dank, musty places I truly wish I hadn't gone, and I work hard to manage that, but it's also a part of *who I am now*. I'm certainly flawed and my biggest flaw turns out to be one of my greatest gifts. Could one of your own flaws actually be a gift? What do you consider an enemy in yourself? If you switched perspectives, like I did, could it all look different?

I learned something when I was told I was my own worst enemy. As hard as it was at the time, I think the words were a favor, even as they hurt me more than any other words ever have. Sometimes misfortune is really just fortune wearing different clothes. God sends trials to teach us lessons. Heartache is just love disguised, maybe. What could feel like words or situations meant to hurt us (and sometimes, maybe they *are* actually said or done to hurt us) often have an unexpected or unintended result. They are quite often the very thing that makes us reach a breakthrough, and that summer, I reached one. I needed to, but the self-reflection was really hard. It made me think, long and hard, about *that world within*, and the enemies I've ensnared myself in. It hurt the way a thorn does on a rose stem, the way you can hardly ever get to a rose without getting pricked by the sharp thorns, protectors of the beauty, and I had work to do.

Oddly, gardening helped me. I took it up that summer, something I never really thought I'd do. While I've always savored fresh flowers, and grew up in the country, I've never been much of a gardener. When I was a little girl, I'd watch my mom tirelessly work with her tiny spade and her gloves. She'd quietly work on the bank of the hill we lived on as I played in the yard or entertained myself on the swing. She would work, her hands toiling in the dirt, and I have always enjoyed the reward of her work: flowers. Now I know it was a way to relax for her then, as it's become for me.

One morning, the wind was blowing perfectly, the sun bright but the temperature low for a summer day in Pennsylvania, and I decided I'd pull a few weeds while my children drew on the driveway with sidewalk chalk. What started with a few weeds quickly turned into an obsession: to make the flower beds here beautiful like I'm sure they once were. I'm not sure I've ever done more satisfying work than what I did that summer, weed by weed. I remember actually talking to the weeds and to the flowers, telling the pink peonies my husband dug up for me from our old house and planted here that I was going to set them free from the poison vine wrapped around them. I put on a jean shirt and gloves to protect myself from the poison (and got it on my arm anyway) and pulled it from them. Grapevine had also infiltrated, coiled tightly around my beloved lilac bush— *how dare it?*—and I found myself passionate to untangle the lilac bush. The grapevine was gnarly and had formed perfect coils around the lilac branches. *No, not on what will become my beautiful purple flowers.*

Weeds became the enemy to me, to the blooms, to the glory and promise the flowers were and are to me. Gardening maybe wasn't something I'd ever really considered doing, but maybe it was because I myself had been entangled in weeds, on and off, for a long time. I myself needed to be set free.

Finally, after all these years, I needed to accept *who I was now*, who I was made to be. Weeds were what was preventing the flowers from fully blooming, preventing the world from seeing, in total, the beauty of the flowers. That's like us, isn't it? Maybe our enemy might be the weeds we entangle *ourselves* in—*too this, too that, not enough here, too much here, too little here.* Maybe our enemy is really the fact that we fail to *accept ourselves*—our serious nature, our unorganized desks and calendars, our need sometimes to hide away, the not-so-flat stomachs, the thighs that touch, the gray hairs, the wrinkles. Maybe the holiest thing we can do for ourselves is to love ourselves. Like Parker J. Palmer wrote, "The spiritual life is about becoming more at home in your own skin."[1] It's so simple but, really, I guess it feels pretty radical. This is self-talk, too, and it's helped me to watch how the others we share the earth with do things.

One morning, like most mornings, I walked outside with my coffee to the sound of a woodpecker. Diligently he pecked, as I scanned the woods behind our house for his familiar red head. His persistence always has impressed me. No matter the weather, he pecks because he's just so certain he is here to do that. Have you noticed how animals never question their purpose? Owls hoot. Dogs bark. Turkeys strut. Crows caw. Woodpeckers peck. Our chickens lay their eggs. Our ducks swim. And yet we spend so much time questioning our own purposes instead of simply doing what we're here to do. Maybe in the routine of our lives, our real purpose is revealed. Maybe life doesn't have to be lived in thick brushstrokes, all paint laden, like I used to think, but in the simple, small stroke of a pen, like the pen and ink lines I once watched my father make, quickly sometimes and slowly at other times, but always turning into a drawing of a deer or a fox, a tree or a flower. Animals don't constantly question their every move, criticizing themselves at every turn, considering their place in things. They know their gifts easily, quickly. We do, too, I think. But we forget, we lose our way, we veer off, we allow ourselves to be led astray, and then our gifts are lost—our callings just something we barely remember. An old photo reminded me of mine, actually.

One night, I stumbled across an old photo in a book I pulled from my shelf. The photo was from 1999, taken before digital photography or iPhone photos. I am in the photo with my dear friend, and we are in England. And there, in that photo, I was a writer, and even though I never called myself one out loud, I felt like one. On our study-abroad trip, I spent hours on trains traveling from London to Edinburgh, Manchester to York, and I mostly just watched people and, inspired by the landscape, wrote pages and pages about it. I had so many story ideas. The weather spoke to me—the rain and the gloom—and I simply embraced it for what it was, growing to love it, which is something I quickly lost the ability to do later about weather and about myself. Back then, I was introspective and connected to myself in ways I hadn't been since childhood, and my friend loved and accepted me in ways only kindred spirits can.

I boarded a plane back to the United States and lost confidence in my writing and myself and packed the journals away in a box. I almost think I packed a large part of myself up in that box too. They stayed there for almost nineteen years. I stopped writing altogether and threw myself into finishing school, then into becoming a wife, teacher, and then mother—the setting up of a life I've treasured. But I left behind a core part of my identity, there in the journals in the box.

But all these years later, after much work, heartbreak, and soul-searching, maybe I'm finally the girl from that photo, the girl of the life before. When I look at her, it's almost like welcoming in an old friend. *Hi, Kara, my dear old friend. I'm so glad you're here. Come, join me on this sofa. I'll make you your favorite tea, the kind you've forgotten about, English breakfast with cream and vanilla, topped with whipped cream.* I was content to be right where I was, and while I don't regret what I did after the photo was taken—I've been told that regret does us no good, after all—I do wish I hadn't abandoned my writing and the path I found myself on. I turned my back on who I was in the pursuit of who I thought I should be. I thought I should be sure, I should be the best, I should be the thinnest—I should be *right and sure*, in all the ways. Now I remember there's more to me than all that.

There's more to *you* than all that! Maybe accepting *that world within* is about letting go of all that and just accepting we're all works in progress. Can we do that together? Can we simply *be* who we're *meant* to be, right here, right now? Can we accept our worlds within?

⟨⟩

Late one summer day, Matt was building a fort outside, leaves and sticks from the forest behind our house carefully arranged against a tree, forming a lean-to. I told him I thought he was doing a great job and he said, "Thanks, Mom. It's a work in progress." I looked at him and said, "Yes, and we all are." He smiled up at me, his eyes catching the light, his smile all his but all mine at the same time, reflected back to me, literally. His face is his but has its roots in mine; his face is the mirror of the nine-year-old Kara I once was. He was comforted by the fact, I think, that there were no expectations of perfection for him, and his smile reminded me of the same about me.

Here, with my people, I'm not expected to do it all "right." No one here is expected to be anyone or anything other than *who they are*, and if someone expects perfection, we are all learning that such a thing doesn't exist, not here in this house, not anywhere, and so we calmly gaze at each other and get on with the work of being imperfect. In our family, here in the house on the hill, like Brené Brown has said, are "the gifts of imperfection,"[2] right in one another's faces. I know that now and Mike does, too, and because of that, our kids know it too.

I am starting to accept *who I am now*, that world within. I might forget the due date for the kids' school book order, but I throw a mean Valentine's Day classroom party (complete with cupid floats!). I'm sometimes late to places, but I'm the mom who watches in awe as snowflakes fall on the eyelashes of my children. I might overthink my relationships at times, but I'm a good friend who tries hard to live up to the friendships I've been blessed with. Bedtimes are variable for my kids because I know well the need for a spontaneous dance party to "Get Back" by the Beatles, and I love to dance, even though I'm terrible at it. My jeans are sometimes too tight and I have tried hard to stop obsessing about calories and instead shift my focus to health. It's not always easy, but in the end, it's pretty simple: *I love chocolate too much to walk away from it.* I sometimes say the wrong thing, speak too quickly or without thought, or I misstep in so many other ways, but I've learned the value of a heartfelt apology and grace received from my people and from my Maker. And the truth is: I'm loved despite my flaws. *You're* loved despite *your* flaws.

My physical appearance has changed, but I'm trying to accept this body and the comfort it can be and the work it can do. I'm learning to eat the bread and the spaghetti sometimes but, at the same time, try to get my time in on the elliptical and run with the kids in the yard and hike like I used to in the woods. Like a friend told me recently while we were in line for a spaghetti dinner at a local amusement park, "We are healthy. Let's just eat the spaghetti." *Yes.* Let's! Please, let's! I run to another friend's classroom between classes for dark chocolate and I rarely feel shame anymore. Imagine! No shame! I have gray hairs that pop up now in my dark brown hair, and while I do color my hair from time to time, look closely and you'll see them. I have age spots and wrinkles around my eyes, and sometimes I go for months without eye cream and I very rarely wear foundation. It all just is what it is.

I suffer from anxiety and depression and while I'm working hard on both, maybe they'll never leave me totally. Maybe it doesn't work that way and I'm learning to live with them, the way I did with roommates in college. I'm learning to accept and claim who I am instead of constantly being embarrassed internally while seeming so confident externally. The "all sure and all figured out" costume has come off, and sometimes that looks like running into my kids' school in my sweats, with my cup of coffee forgotten in my hand, and running into the most stylish mom I know, in the most beautiful clothes, but stopping and talking to her, my hair piled on top of my head, a colorful wrap covering my hair that needs to be washed. It's about seeing others and not wanting their lives or comparing myself to them. I like my own life. I like the fact that I don't feel embarrassed wearing a Nirvana T-shirt and ripped jeans with my favorite Birkenstocks. It's who I am now. *It's who I've always been.*

Once, when Maggie and Matt were playing outside, Maggie fell. She came to me and wanted me to hold her. This happens from time to time and like every other time, that day, like I once did when she was a baby, I wrapped her in a pink blanket my Meemom crocheted for her, and held her tight, everything but her face covered. She looked up at me and I stared back at her and she stopped crying, comforted in my arms and with my eyes. When my children were babies, both of them loved to stare at my face, memorizing it, I guess. Maggie and I once did this time on end, and back then, I feared I was doing it all wrong, just like I had with her brother. I wondered the same thing that day and every day since. *Am I doing this all wrong? Like, all of it? Life and all? I am doing all of it wrong? What will she remember about me? How is she this big, and me, how am I still this unsure? Have I done right by her? Will I do right by her? Is she even going to like me when she's the age of the girls I teach? Am I enough for her or this or anything else?* I stared at her and she stared at me; my green eyes have finally met their match in her blue ones. And then she smiled and I smiled and my soul sighed a sigh of relief. Like 1 Samuel 3:4, "Here I am," now.

Here I am now. I'm starting to accept my flaws and insecurities while working on them all. I accept my serious nature and the double-checking of the coffeepot and curling iron. I have a complete disdain for spreadsheets, calendars, schedules, and timelines (I can't pretend anymore!), but I love nature, children, and animals. I don't like going to the dentist, at all, but I'm a good person to check in on *you* after an appointment of any sort. I usually remember. I love people but often like to be alone, and that confuses even me sometimes. We entertain on the regular here and while I was once a hot mess the day before people came over, as I rushed to make everything just *right*, I know now no one cares. My windows are often dirty because the dog jumps up on the ledges all the time to admire the view. *Here we are.* Let's try hard to see the good in who we are because it is one way to welcome an everywhere holy. I'm still a work in progress but I think that will be lifelong. Many of us still have work to do. I sure do. But *I'm on my way.*

Here's what I want to say to you: *Accept your world within.* You must remember you are a gift from God, made by God. There are gifts in this person you've become. Let us give thanks for fresh starts, with the sun on the horizon. A good friend texted me after I put myself down to her about this whole process—the process of *accepting this world within*—and how my overthinking had gotten the best of me. She simply said, "I like you the way you are." Thank you, my friend. Let us thank God for our people who help us learn how to accept *ourselves* as we are, and in turn, we can accept them *as they are.* It's reciprocal, beautiful, holy. Thank you, God, for sending people to teach us lessons, even through the pain. It's hard but we're learning to be grateful, even for the difficult things. Let us give thanks for the people put in our paths who allow us to begin again and accept us with our mistakes and our faults.

In the photo I found from 1999 is Kara, the overthinker, the feeler, the writer, the watcher, the lover of nature, side by side with a friend who has loved her for who she is, even from afar, for all these years. I wasn't in competition with myself or anyone else. Back then, I had nothing to prove.

There is Kara before she decided to be someone she's not. There she is and *here I am*. Like Kate Chopin wrote in *The Awakening*, "She was becoming herself and daily casting aside that fictitious self which we assume like a garment with which to appear before the world."[3] I've cast aside that fictitious self.

Now it's your turn. It's really time to accept who you are; it's time to put away the face that's not your own. Put the costume—that *not-you* disguise—away, once and for all, and simply love your own face. As for me, I am who I was *then*, finally, *again*?

Sometimes, when I look out the window above my kitchen sink to the woods, the trees play tricks on me. The fallen trees and stumps, clusters of bushes and brush, give the illusion of something other than what's there. The blackness through the trees reminds me of a bear and, once, I thought it was only a tree cluster, but it really was a bear, slowly moving through the forest behind our home. She had cubs and I ran, waving my arms, and calling the kids in quickly but quietly from their blue swing by the tree line, for we all know we must be careful around mama bears. It was gloomy, like it often is here on the mountainside, the fog never going away on some days. Today, I looked and I thought the bear was back, but she wasn't. It was just the trees playing tricks on me.

I wonder if our eyes play tricks on us sometimes—the way we see ourselves in the mirror is different from the way others see us. I wonder if words play tricks on us—the way

I allowed myself to believe I was my own enemy and spin it into so much negative self-talk. It's like the trees playing tricks on me, the thicket too confusing to see through at times, snakes where there are none. But when our eyes adjust, the shapes come into focus; the reality of who or what is in front of us also comes into focus. When we can begin to accept ourselves, it all becomes a bit clearer—the layers and intricacies of who we are make more sense, and just like how we begin to realize and recognize the beauty in the forest, we also recognize the beauty in us all. *We are not our own enemies.* Yes, we're flawed and maybe we even have work to do. But we cannot be pitted against ourselves, the (imaginary?) snakes hissing, waiting to strike, venomous and ready. *We are not our own enemies.* We are *chosen, created, beloved.*

Finally, maybe I can *accept who I am now*, this very second, minute, hour, day, year, and maybe you can too. In the end, I'm not sure there's anything holier than that. An everywhere holy can seep into the places we feel not good enough and allow our souls to sigh a sigh of relief, leaving us with the feeling of acceptance for *our world within*, if we only let it.

CHAPTER 13

Life Less Difficult

"What do we live for, if it is not to make
life less difficult for each other?"
—George Eliot (Mary Ann
Evans), *Middlemarch*

A friend once invited me to a spiritual yoga class, and on a Sunday evening in midwinter, I met her there. I hadn't been to yoga in a very long time and I had forgotten much of what I once knew, long ago. It was a room full of only women, the soft yellow glow of candles all around, a gathering of faces cast in shadows. I was struck by the candles as soon as I entered the room, the way they reminded me of the ones in a cathedral, flickering on faces, holy. We went through various yoga poses, the breathing of *in and out, in and out* that took me some time to remember, the breathing not as natural for me now, the moves unfamiliar again, many of which were harder than I'd remembered.

Toward the end of the yoga class, the yoga instructor had us do something I don't ever remember doing almost twenty years ago when I went to yoga with my mom: she had us stand and balance on one leg, holding our arms out to our sides, palms pointed up, there to catch another woman if needed. It was a balancing I found hard to do, faltering a bit, swaying from side to side. As I struggled to find my balance on my own, my palm touched the palm of my friend and I was secured, standing upright, unwavering because of the strength I found in her palm. When I swayed, her palm was there to catch me, and when she swayed, my palm and the palm of her other friend beside her caught her. I watched the rows of women—one in front of me, and one behind—and each woman was strength for the woman beside her. The strength in the room was palpable to me, each of us made strong by one another, in a chain of sorts, palm to palm. Women lifting up other women, palm to palm, preventing a fall, making the pose less difficult. It reminded me then of a passage in the Bible.

To summarize briefly, in Exodus 17:10–13, Joshua and the Israelites were battling the Amalekites, but as long as

Moses held up his hands with the rod of God, the Israelites maintained the winning position. As long as his arms were up, the battle raged in their favor. Of course, as we all would after hours of holding our arms up, Moses grew tired and could no longer hold up his own arms. But others came to his rescue, holding up his arms for him, keeping his hands high with the rod. They swooped in and steadied him, holding him up, allowing the war to be won.

Sometimes, life itself can feel like a battle and we find ourselves swaying from side to side. We might feel alone, as if we carry the weight of *all of it* on our shoulders. We forget how to breathe *in and out* and instead our breathing becomes frantic, unsettled, the air choking in our lungs. Sometimes it feels like we're losing at *all of it*, all of the things, and we focus on all the ways we wish we were but aren't, all the things we wish we did but didn't. We stumble, trip, and crumble under the weight. Maybe we find ourselves feeling sad and alone and like we are failing at it all. I know I've felt this way before, less these days than before, but from time to time, the feelings still wash over me like waves, surprising me, causing me to stumble, and sometimes, I lose my footing. There are days I simply feel like I can't hold my arms up anymore; I can't keep them stretched out at my sides; I simply cannot stand on one leg any longer. I forget how to breathe *in and out, in and out*. I falter and then I almost fall, but like Mark Nepo wrote in *The Book of Awakening*, I look up and see others around me:

We wander and think no one will ever find us.
And lifting our sorry head,
we are next to each other.[1]

I'm reminded of the time in the yoga studio that winter night and of the Exodus passage, this holding up of arms and hands, this ultimate act of friendship and hand-holding, this healing, this *I will hold you even when you cannot hold yourself* type of rescuing, this standing alongside, the reminder to breathe, *in and out*. I used to think this was only the work of family and the best of friends, the very rare friends who become our family. I once didn't understand how strangers or relative strangers can be this for one another. But now I see it differently. Now I know that if we keep our arms outstretched, our palms out, it can be found in a group of women on a random winter night in the glow of the yoga studio or as a text across the screen of my phone from an acquaintance that says, "Checking in." I know now that it's in the Shasta daisies I have in the garden out back, picked and given to a friend. I know now that it happens randomly, like the time I heard from a reader of my writing. She messaged me about a very sick family member and asked for prayers. I rallied the group that is my online social media community. I'd never met her but I wanted to steady her hand, help her balance on one leg, help her breathe *in and out*, and in doing so, I saw all the women rally, all the women reach across time and space, palms held out to the side like we do when we say the "Our Father" prayer. And it wasn't the first nor will it be the last time hands reached across cyberspace.

One afternoon, I had just a bit of time alone and found myself at the monastery close to my home. The grounds are truly beautiful there and my goal was to admire the perfect view of the mountains by the statue of Mary. For five minutes, I just wanted to sit there with her in the sun. I walked through the parking lot to the road and waited for traffic to pass so I could cross. One by one, cars blazed by and that seemed odd to me, as I've always thought of it as a quiet road. I waited and waited for the cars to go by and used my waiting opportunity to look to the left and to the right.

As I waited, I noticed a trail across the road and to my right, tall evergreens lining a path. I'd never seen it before, although I'm sure that was because I was always rushing, never paying attention, quickly running to the gift shop there, in and out. The closer I got, the more I could see it was an aisle. I didn't have much time, but I turned toward the path and decided I'd go there first, under the canopy of trees, the sun only peeking through the tops. I walked, suddenly sure of the direction I would go and in what order: first to the trees and then to admire the mountain view by Mary. I walked there only because there was a call of the familiar, a whisper on the breeze, a beckon. I walked and breathed deep when I saw what the woodland aisle led to: a wooden cross, simple and imperfect. It surprised me for some reason. I was at a monastery, after all, so I really shouldn't have been at all surprised by the cross. But this rudimentary cross, in its simplicity, with rocks at the bottom, at the end of a wooded path, really did make me pause. I stood at the end of the aisle, the trees providing almost complete shade from the sun, and stared. It moved me that much—the image of it, the quiet, the breeze, and the single ray of sunshine from above peeking through the canopy. I gazed up at the sun, shining for sure, but only one ray streaming into this holy of holiest spaces. The trees were so tall and it was clear they'd been there forever, and I imagined all who had stood there, in awe, like I was. I stood and reached my right hand up to the light. Then I walked slowly to the foot of the cross.

As I was walking, a name of a woman I don't know well popped into my head, someone I'd met years prior at a local Halloween parade. This was before Maggie was born, and our boys were around the same age, interested in one another, and so she and I talked a bit. I instantly liked her then, I remember, but she moved away and we only became friends on social media. In the weeks before my day there at the monastery, I'd seen her post things online and it was clear to me from them that she was going through a journey of her own. While I was sure our paths were different, maybe even in some great and profound ways, it did seem our goal was the same: searching for the light, walking on the path. For some reason, it was her name that came to my mind as I walked to the cross. I quickly took a photo of the cross and without giving it much thought, I sent it to her, a hand reached across the space that is social media, a palm up but a head bowed, arms outstretched. It was an impulsive move, a risk of seeming ridiculous I quickly realized as soon as I hit send, but I sent the photo, and minutes later, she replied and thanked me for sending it. She pondered, on the page, how I could know her so well and I didn't say it to her there, but I thought it: *it's because I'm on the same journey.*

And while our journeys maybe aren't the exact same in the steps or even in navigation, aren't we *all* just reaching for the light, doing our very best to walk the path laid out for us? Aren't we more the same than we are different as we practice the *holy art of breathing*? *In and out, in and out.* Aren't we *all* simply doing this, day to day, simply breathing *in and out* on some days, looking for some light in an otherwise dark world? Like the cross, imperfect? Aren't we just looking for the single ray of sunshine? The beauty in the darkness that is the shade from the trees? The cross, strong but dirty? Isn't it what we all want to see?

The single beam of light through the trees—solitary if it is all we have on our own but we, together with the other "warriors of light,"[2] like Paulo Coelho calls us in the 2002 introduction to *The Alchemist*, join our rays together until we are so bright. That's what my hand reaching was, and even if it might not have been that for *her*, it really was for *me*. Like Saint Francis wrote, "It is in giving that we receive."[3] The hand extended, my single ray of light hoping to reach hers, but the light was reflected back to me. The gathering of light, really, the idea that we really are women together, steadying one another with our palms, fingers pointed upward. In the end, it's the holding up of one another that keeps us standing, breathing.

I stood and stared, prayed, bowed my head, and then I walked onward to the view of the mountains. I sat and simply breathed, *in and out, in and out, in and out*, my chest rising and falling, the deep stomach breaths I learned from my long-gone days of singing, back when doing so didn't embarrass me, the ones I also used in yoga years ago and just this past winter, again. The sun shone brightly on my face, the mountain my view, so very green and lovely, really, with the promise of spring and new beginnings. I sat and I breathed; that's all I did, legs crossed in front of a peeling birch tree, branches strewn all around from a storm, the white bark in contrast to the green grass but all of it a reminder of life. The cross visible to me from the backside now, the aisle magical, the air spectacular, the sun on my face, the weight on my chest temporarily relieved because my palm perhaps reached someone else's and in doing so, my arms were held up, just like Moses, just like the women that night in the yoga studio. *In and out, in and out.*

We will breathe *in and out, in and out*, choosing breath and our *own life*, and like that day at the monastery, we will get up and we will walk, one foot in front of the other. Later, we might hear from another of their own suffering—even small trials—and we will look up from staring downward, downtrodden, and reach out for them, too, until it's a chain of so many women, palm to palm, just like the yoga studio, just like Exodus, just like the women across cyberspace. The palms will steady us and we won't let go and it'll be our *own* prayer: *Here, let me steady you. Let me hold you. Breathe with me, in and out, in and out.* It's hard but I will hold you and you will hold me and we will hold fast to this life, for *it is enough.* And it will *be* enough. For really, what's holier than breathing in and out? The action, the dare to take one breath after another and continue on in the life God laid for us? Truly, *what's holier than living?* Together, we breathe, in and out. We steady one another, making life less difficult. We become like the people who held Moses. We are everywhere holy, *together*, palm to palm.

CHAPTER 14

A Language Without Words

Perhaps there is a language which
is not made of words.

—Frances Hodgson Burnett,

A Little Princess

It's been quite a journey but now, if I listen, I really can hear a holy language without words everywhere, all around, in the beauty around me, in my people, and now, finally, even in me. The way of the Jesuits is to search for "God in all things,"[1] and I do now. I've seen this holiness everywhere and *in* everything—the way my daughter's face lights up in the sun while I fill the car with gas at the gas station, the dance of the honeybees my dad loves so much who flock to the clover, the magic that spreads across my son's face when he hugs his dog, the laughing I observe while watching my husband and son play a game of catch in our yard, the way my mom talks lovingly about her best friend who died too young. It's not a voice as much as it is the observation of my life, and that observation has become a form of prayer to me—the best form of prayer I've found yet—but it wasn't always that way for me.

Over the years, on occasion, I heard a language without words, but it wasn't at all something that I'd acknowledge daily. Sure, I'd hear it on the breeze when I sat alone on the beach while my husband was stationed in the South. I'd feel it when we drove home to see our families and passed through Cowans Gap State Park, where the mountains spoke to my soul, which was so desperate to see them. But it wasn't until I became a mother and saw the world through the eyes of my children that, over time, I relearned how to pay attention. I have learned to listen again to that language without words.

The wiping of hands and faces can feel sacred and the walk through the fields reminds me of who I am again; through all of this, holiness comes to me in a hushed language—hardly audible if I'm not listening closely enough. But as I've learned to listen, it whispers of a simple holy, tangible, real. While my life is perhaps an ordinary one by most standards, it's a life well lived. It's the revelation of identity; it's beauty from pain. An everywhere holy has been revealed to me in my ritual of life—making coffee, washing eggs, talking to other parents, teaching high schoolers, gardening, tending animals, doing dishes, bathing children. And it was a few years ago, when I gave my son a bath, when that language without words whispered right in the mess of the bathroom.

Matt is no longer a baby or toddler or even a young boy. He's up to my shoulder now and so gone are the days of bathing him, but when he was little, I'd put him in his little blue tub and carefully wash each arm and leg. He was so chubby I'd have to be sure to get in between the rolls of skin on his neck. He'd giggle, gums revealed, as I sang to him and bathed him, relishing the smell of lavender baby wash my sister used to use on her children too. He was my baby and I took good care of him.

A few years ago, he was sick with a stomach bug. He desperately needed a bath, but he was too weak to bathe himself. As I washed his hands and his back, I took note of how big his hands were—they stretched well beyond the middle joints of my fingers, and are now, years later, almost as big as mine, and it won't be long until they overtake my own. His back was lean, suddenly it seemed—all rib cage and muscle. Gone were the rolls of skin on his neck. I poured cup after cup of water over his back and remembered how, when he was a baby, the pouring of water relaxed him so much; he'd close his eyes as if he were going to fall asleep. I closed my eyes and prayed right there, right in the ordinariness of the bathroom. As I poured the water, I said: *I am here and grateful for this child.* When I looked at him, his eyes were closed too. It was a quiet and rather ordinary moment, but it was holy, right in that moment of bathing a boy whom I had held the bucket for when he was sick just an hour before. My life said, "This, this is where you are to be." And even as it might have looked like the unholiest of places—a grimy bathroom with residual stomach flu on a dark night in winter, I was reminded of Jesus washing the feet of his disciples and of the baptisms of my children, their heads held over water as they were ceremoniously cleansed. I know God was there in the bathroom that very night, helping me mother my sick child and guiding me in mothering the holy moments I encounter in the simplest of places, like the bathroom or the woods near our house, if I listen for the language without words. It might not always be easy, but it is a start.

One afternoon in a past summer, we set out after dinner with galvanized buckets to pick black raspberries from the many bushes at our house. Mike loves to bake and can, and our goal was to make jam and pies. We needed many berries, and we had a lot of picking ahead of us. Matt led the way to the ripest bushes, as he had already picked some for his afternoon snack earlier the same day.

We picked and picked and Maggie ate many more than she picked. With her small but no-longer-baby hands dyed red, I watched her eat one after the other from the bucket in her hand—the one her brother kept filling for her, without complaint. She was suddenly talking so much then and I caught myself simply staring at her when I should've been picking berries myself. She was just newly three. As I watched her chatter on, eating raspberries in her oversize, bright-pink sunhat from my aunt Tracy, I vowed never to forget the moment.

Sometimes I think if I stare long enough, how could I ever forget? I stare a lot as a result. Surely I'll remember the color of the raspberries in her growing hands, the bright pink of her hat and boots? Surely I'll remember how her brother doted on her, bending down to show her where a plump black raspberry was, well within her reach? Surely I'll remember his eight-year-old voice praising her and the hug she gave him in return? The acknowledgment of these holy moments—right where they are—is observation prayer.

In the end, that night with the kids was just a small sliver of a full life, but I'm finding the small slices usually are the moments that add up to the full pie of a life worth remembering, all homemade crust, raspberry filled, and oozing a holy goodness. And while there were arguments that day, spilled drinks and snacks, my own lists of tasks left completely undone and bills that needed to be paid, we all really did the raspberry picking thing so perfectly. That night, that hushed language said: *family, family, family.* I found the way God works in my life right there in the raspberry bushes, there as my family picked in the sun that was sinking low behind them, and it was nothing short of holy. While that moment will be one I'll forever remember, it was just an ordinary day at home, one of many. But, in these moments, we are reminded that we're right where we are to be and nothing is by chance, even cats who show up at your country home.

When we moved the previous summer to our rural home, our cat, Lily, naturally came with us. We had considered adopting another cat from our local SPCA, but we planned to wait a while before adding more animals to our home. In late January of our first winter, there was a big snowstorm, and we all reveled in the snow covering the mountain view in front of us—the stunning, snowcapped purples like gumdrops. After the kids were bathed, we sat on the sofa to watch the snow fall from the tall windows in our living room. It was during this snow that Mike saw a small calico outside.

When he first spotted her, he was shoveling our walkway and he bent down and she walked over to him. He came in and told us about her and as he did, we looked out on the porch and there she was, sitting at our window, looking in. We opened the window and we all petted her before Matt noticed the unusual markings. "She has a cross on her face," he said. And lo and behold, she did. She had a cross of sorts on her face, in bright peach, and she had arrived in the dead of winter with nowhere to go, no place to call home. We named her Mary.

The kids checked on her that first night about ten times, and I put her in a basket with blankets as Mike asked around to see if she belonged to someone. He said to me that night, "Boy, you really like her," and that was very true. When I was a little girl, I had a cat that looked so much like her. Emotional and sentimental, I stared at her and my eyes filled with tears at the memories of my life with Sis, our cat, at my childhood home. Even Mike remembers her from all those years ago, when he and I were both just kids and we'd sit outside at my old house under the stars with Sis in my lap.

Perhaps I could look at that as all coincidental, but I know now that the language without words visits us in unlikely ways. In the end, this tiny calico cat belonged to no one but us. I've learned so many lessons through Mary since we've had her; she was meant to be our cat and I think I was meant to be her mother.

Shortly after she arrived, before we knew for sure if she would stay and before we could get her spayed, we found out rather quickly she was pregnant. We all observed the growing belly and the kids marveled at the small cat whose belly blossomed quickly, and as time went on, it was clear to me she would have the kittens any day.

Late one Sunday afternoon, before daylight saving time and "spring forward," she walked out of the woods and her large belly was completely gone. She had given birth somewhere in the dense forest behind our home. Mike put his boots on and set off into the thicket to see if he could find the kittens before dusk, as they would be easy prey for the coyotes we often hear howling at night or maybe even for the occasional bear we see, one once running down our driveway, with food from our trash trailing from its mouth. Mike searched and when he returned, he didn't have any kittens. As we talked about our next steps, we heard thunder from a storm that was quickly rolling in. Matt and Maggie started to cry, completely overcome with worry for the kittens in the woods. Mike wasn't sure what else to do and I simply stood up and said, "I think I know where they are." He joked and said, "How? I just looked!" My simple reply was "I'm a mother," to which he rolled his eyes.

I have to tell you it was one of the strangest moments of my life. I stood up, climbed our retaining wall, and simply walked into the woods to the foot of one of many, many trees. A bush had taken over its base, and nestled in the bush were five tiny kittens. In that moment, somehow, I guessed where they were.

We moved the kittens to our garage, where our cats sleep on heated beds, and Mary tended them in the best ways I've ever seen any mother tend her newborn. The kittens stayed with us for eight weeks before they were successfully adopted into loving homes, but not before my children made memories they'll remember forever. I won't ever forget how the gray kitten almost matched my son's eyes perfectly or how the orange one's fur was the same honey color as Maggie's hair. I won't forget the research Matt did on the biological chance that Mary had no kittens that looked like her. Not even one kitten looked like Mary! I won't forget a kitten climbing up my leg or my husband posing for a photo my daughter insisted on, his lap filled with kittens. We all made memories we will treasure forever. And while the holy beauty reveals itself to me in these experiences, of course, sometimes it's through the literal words of others that I hear it if I simply listen.

One winter afternoon, I took Matt to a poetry reading and workshop. It was for my own high school students, but he wanted to go and, mostly, I am happy for the times when he still wants to tag along with me. I'll admit that on that particular day, after a morning of him teasing his sister too much, I wanted to drive alone and sit alone and listen alone, without a child to care for. And yet I took him because he truly wanted to be with me, and I'm so glad I did because holy took on the shape of words to me that day, loud and clear.

Matt listened to the reading, eating a chocolate bar as he did (he is my son, after all). When it came time for the workshop part, he asked me if he could join in. The poet is a friend of mine whom he'd known for years and when he asked to participate, too, she quickly obliged. He sat with a magazine photo like everyone else. His photo was of a woman with two children, a soccer ball exiting the photo to the left.

My friend led a series of activities and Matt wrote out complete sentences in response to them. I walked around the room, reading and watching some of my own students write, chatting with my poet friend as the creativity became palpable in the room. I checked in on Matt, but he largely set to work, focused on the photo and the words he spilled onto the page. He was busy and I sipped my tea for a while, content to watch everyone work.

When I returned to see the almost final product of Matt's, "On a Playground," it took my breath away. Here is the final, polished product he completed that day. Matt, then only seven, wrote:

> On a playground
> My mother's hands hold mine.
> My hair swings in the air.
> The excitement of other people is all around.
> The wind blows and the air is fresh.
> The leaves of the trees.
> The salt in the air.
> The hair on my face.
> On a playground
> My mother's hands hold mine.
>
> —MATT, AGE SEVEN

When I read it, he put his arms around my waist and watched me in expectation. When I told him how much I loved it, his face glowed with pride, and he said, "Thanks, Mom. I knew you would."

If I hadn't taken him that day, I would never have known the beauty of this poem I will simply treasure forever, reminding me of the importance of my role as a mother to one small boy who still thought every story began with me. Often, it's through my children and the children of others that I hear holy whispers in that language without words.

We had friends over, their children and our children becoming more and more like cousins as time passes. They hugged one another and Maggie told Matt's best friend, "I love you." They're becoming to one another like some family friends were to me when I was growing up: a constant, and I'm grateful for it. Now I see the same relationship forming between my own children and the children of our friends. We were all hanging out and talking, the conversations coming easy now, laughing the norm as the kids played behind us, close to the tree line. They were digging in the ground, searching for rocks and "maybe even a fossil," I heard a voice exclaim. They spent an hour making a rudimentary stone table, makeshift but purposeful, a table for them, right by the tall oak, right by the wood's edge. They each selected a rock as their seat and I ran up to my bathroom. As I sat down to go to the bathroom (glamorous, I know), I heard their chitter-chatter from the open window.

They told one another to sit down and their voices gathered until I heard them—all four in unison—begin to recite the "Our Father" prayer. I listened, captivated by the child voices, the children I love, the simple and make-believe meal they were preparing for at their stone table, right in the middle of it all. After they finished the prayer, I heard Matt tack on one extra prayer. He said, "Thank you, God, for this day and for this food." I was literally in the bathroom, on the toilet, but their words drifted in the bathroom window on a breeze and I marveled at this simple confirmation of God, alive and well, in the hearts of the children sitting at a stone table. Holy spoke, right then and there. Other times, I'll admit: it's not as easy to see or hear.

On some days, I feel like all I'm doing is logging time

and telling my kids to stop arguing, and some days might seem unremarkable by most accounts if I'm not careful. But then Maggie puts her small hands to her mouth, and in one perfect moment, she blows me a kiss. Another glimpse of glory. Holy, holy, holy. Glory free for the taking, fleeting but *true*. Glory whispers and even shouts and then all of it comes tumbling back: Matt, asleep, who woke to my kiss on his head. A quick coffee with a friend. Students who loved the poem I read in class. Deer nestled in the thicket as geese flew overhead. A whip-poor-will in the tree. A seafoam-green chicken egg. A cat brushing against my leg. Chickens running to me for their snacks of tomatoes. Mike squeezing my hand.

Holiness reveals itself as we see our very own lives as *enough*, even amid the struggle and the heaviness that some days bring. It's there—the glory, I mean. If we're not careful, we might not notice, but it's there, truer than true. And in the end, there's nothing ordinary about it, and I was reminded on a drive home from my parents' house, a reminder that holy moments might not look the way we imagine.

One early summer evening, we took the long way home from the small town my parents live in to our home on the outskirts of another small town, thirty minutes away. The Jeep top was off and the fresh air blew my hair all around. Because the wind was blowing, everyone was quiet and looking out at the nature sprawled before us. We all have learned to live for nights like this—long Jeep rides on winding roads, all sunshine and air. I took in the sights—the regal beauty of the sun fading, but also of the truck bench and of the white plastic chairs discarded by the river. They were ugly at first glance, maybe, but a reminder to me that people sit there and enjoy the river, and that is a beautiful image.

We turned a corner and I saw a hand-painted Beware of Dog sign and laughed when I saw it was actually a painting of a basset hound. Mike pulled into a convenience store for a coffee and we parked next to an old man in an old car, his arms covered in old and fading tattoos. I looked at him and he looked at me and his crystal-blue eyes caught me off guard, familiar somehow. *How?* I smiled and he smiled back before taking another puff of his cigarette, smoke billowing.

We continued our journey home and passed women rocking on front porch rockers and they were laughing together—friends or sisters, perhaps, and they made me smile too. My husband put on an Avett Brothers song and my son started to sing it; he was loud, confident, sure, and I turned to look at him, grateful, his hair blowing in the wind, too, and we smiled at one another and kept singing. Ordinary but holy, just like later that night in my chicken coop.

It was almost dark when I looked out the window to see the lights on in our chicken coop. It's a small building—an 8' x 10' structure—one I saw on Pinterest and Mike built for me the first full summer we lived in this house on the hill. It has board and batten siding, painted white, with an arched door I love. When I saw the lights on, I also saw the door slightly ajar, left open by my children who were in there playing with Sunny, the newest baby chick Matt hatched in his second-grade science classroom in an incubator. I grabbed a flashlight, put on my black rubber boots, and walked across the yard to the open door.

The chickens were all on the roost—a mantel we salvaged from the trash pile of an old house undergoing renovation. Our coop is perhaps too fancy, with its thirty-nine-dollar IKEA chandelier and all, but it seems to suit my hens just fine. They were back behind the huge, old window Mike used to make a wall to separate the babies from the full-grown hens. The babies all rushed to me and a few chickens left the roost to go to the door. They seemed to be waiting for the nighttime ritual, the petting of them Mike had told me about but I'd never done. They waited and I walked in to pet them, in the hushed yellow light of the coop, the unpainted boards of the inside making the whole building glow like the flickering candles in a cathedral. A sacred moment in a chicken coop, a reminder that this coop on this night with this light, sleeping children in the house, the moon high and bright, is holy enough. Holy enough had reached me that night as I petted the chickens, proving it can be found everywhere, right where we are, right in the smell of a chicken coop.

As I walked back to the house, the dusk shed just enough light for me to make out a silhouette against the mountain. By the big tree I love so much, the one that reveals such glory in the fall, stood a huge buck. His antlers looked majestic, black against the dusk of nightfall. I said, out loud, "Hi, beautiful boy." The words spilled out and were without thought and they surprised me. He and I stared at one another and he moved his head (in a nod?), and I stood, my hands out to him. I said, "The holy in me honors the holy in you," my own variation of "namaste," left over subconsciously, I guess, from a yoga class. I meant it. I really did. He stood and stared and I edged closer, unafraid, as night fell softly all around me. He ran off and I turned to the house, all lit up with the life inside, holy, holy waiting.

As I finish this book, it's only appropriate that both of my children have found their way into our bed. It's early for that, but tonight, as I'm typing in my office right around the corner from our bed, I'm just so thankful for it. I know it won't last forever, so I peek around at them. My daughter's head is resting right on my pillow, her hand outstretched, palm open, like she is waiting for my hand. Her breath is steady like the stars and warm like the sun. She is, to me, *sun and stars*, just like my brother calls his own daughter. My own sun and stars is Maggie, all together in a child who brought light back into my world. Matt, my son, who is like the moon—calm and comforting—a beacon, is next to her with his arm wrapped around her and I can hear his breath too. Mike snores softly, his hand on Matt. Night has fallen and I can hear coyotes and owls through the open window—a whole world outside my window—an everywhere holy if I look and listen. But my whole world is snuggled right in our bed, as I type on the computer, an everywhere holy right in my own people. Now I think I'll rest in the dark as they softly breathe, all three. I think I'll just sit and be still and listen to the night as it falls. The beauty is there and I'm sure of my place in the world, finally. God is right *here*, right now. He's right there with you, right *now*. Holy, holy. I think I hear an everywhere holy.

CHAPTER 15

Me, Just the Same

"I'm not a bit changed—not really. I'm only
just pruned down and branched out. The
real *me*—back here—is just the same."

—LUCY MAUD MONTGOMERY,
ANNE OF GREEN GABLES

One afternoon, right as I was finishing this book, deadline
approaching, I drove down the road near my childhood
home. It was foggy and drizzling—my favorite weather these
days. *Actually, it's always been my favorite weather.* I felt
compelled to drive there, though I tried to ignore it at first.

But I'm learning when I feel strongly about something, it will whisper and then nag before it shouts; it's almost impossible to ignore by then. And it was shouting. I wasn't looking forward to it, really, as for almost a quarter of a century going there has just been a reminder of all I'm not anymore, the Kara I wish I still was. But I drove there, questioning why I had to go, but answering the call, however begrudgingly.

I passed the old barn at the end of the road and one lone cow was in the small pasture. I stopped the car and greeted him, for I've seldom passed the pasture without doing so. I then drove down the dusty road that is newly macadamized in some spots near my childhood home.

I parked the car in the grass just beyond the driveway and muttered as I opened the car door, "Here I am," throwing my hands up in the air. Rather annoyed, I walked up and down the road, the drizzle making spots on my coat. I didn't have a hat and as the rain picked up, my hair became damp. I kept walking, unaffected. I've learned that weather is only weather. I assumed I was there to cross the stream and get to the clearing, once and for all, to find God there like I had all those years ago among the trees, the forest floor the carpet of my dreams. I'd find the old Kara there again, maybe. I walked beyond an old and rusty pump, left from long ago, its purpose never questioned by my child mind, through the fields of land no longer mine, tall with goldenrod and purple field flowers, black-eyed Susans swaying to some unheard song the breeze made. My fingers grazed the tops, my fingertips feeling the memories I'd left there.

When I got to the small creek, I put my rain boot in, a durable and practical black boot, and almost crossed, finally, after all these years, but I realized, quite suddenly, that I had no desire to. I stood there with my foot extended, not touching the water, my arms out to my sides for balance. A realization washed over me as the rain fell faster: I didn't need to get to the clearing anymore. Kara was right here. *I am here. Here I am now.* I stood and stared at the water trickling over a log in the middle before I turned around and walked back to my car. I didn't cry and I didn't hang my head low, like I had every other time I'd been there. I looked up as the rain touched my face and I smiled, lifting my arms again to the sky, and simply said, "Thank you. I understand now. I finally do."

Now I know God isn't just found in the clearing of my youth or on the road by my old house. God isn't only seen in the face of my son as he knelt all in candlelight in Saint Patrick's Cathedral in New York City, his face up, bathing in such a holy light, beautifully and perfectly unforgettable. A holy beauty isn't only spotted in the blue swallowtail butterfly that flew all around me before finally landing on my arm when I was still. God is not only felt when I stare at the cows with my daughter and the breeze blows. And the old Kara is *me*, here, *now*. She's not at my old childhood home. I'm just like I was then, finally, again. I don't need to get to the clearing anymore. I'm not even sure it's there anymore. I'll leave it as it is in my memory—holy, sacred, magical because now I know God is everywhere and I'm who I was, again, the Kara of then. Like Anne says in *Anne of Green Gables*, I can *feel a prayer* wherever I am. The *real me* is remembered. Holiness is found right here, right now. I think I've finally found *everywhere holy*, and I know you can find it too.

Wild, Holy Ground

"You're standing on holy ground."
—EXODUS 3:5

Two weeks after I wrote the last chapter of this book and was in the final editing stages before I sent the manuscript in, Matt finished his lean-to in the woods behind our house. He'd been working on it for months really, gathering branches, sticks, ferns, and moss to create a shelter, a hideout, "maybe even a place to read," he said. It was a Sunday afternoon, cool suddenly, the October beauty I love suddenly upon me, and Matt came in to call me back to see the lean-to and another surprise he told me he had for me.

I put on my black boots and a coat and walked back with him to the woods. Mike had used the Weedwacker to create a path back in the woods to his lean-to and it startled me a bit, as it reminded me of the clearing from my childhood. This *was* a clearing, of sorts, an aisle, the path so wide. The filtered light flickered on Matt's face as he held my hand and asked for me to close my eyes. He guided me back, not far from the house at all, and told me to open my eyes.

There propped up against the tree was a wooden cross he had made last year with Mike out of wood scraps. I'd seen it before and wondered what the new surprise was. I smiled and looked down as he watched my face.

There was one long and flat rock in front of the cross. Stacked in front of it were three rocks, higher. Before I could say anything, Matt knelt down and rested his elbows on the stacked rocks, his hands folded in prayer, the blue, blue sky making its way to his face, and said, "Mom, this is what you do." He had collected rocks in the woods and made me a kneeler, a pew of my own, right there in the wild. He continued, "I made this for you so you can pray back here. I know how much you love the woods and I know the book you're working on is called *Everywhere Holy*."

He stood and I pulled him to me, his hair soft against my face. As I breathed in the smell of him, the musk and wild of the woods, so familiar, and leaves from his lean-to on his flannel shirt, I whispered, "Thank you, Matty. This is the best gift I've ever received." And it is the best gift I've ever received: it was like confirmation to me of all of this, *of all that is holy and true*, all of what's in this book. Holiness is everywhere and now I know, for sure, that it's found me, right here, right where I am. I'm standing on wild, holy ground.

Acknowledgments

"I will only add, God bless you."

—JANE AUSTEN, *PRIDE AND PREJUDICE*

Years ago, in the late 90s at the *Lilith Fair*, I heard Natalie Merchant sing "Kind and Generous," and I fell in love with the song. It was pouring down rain and I was barefoot. It's a memory I'll hold forever. In homage to the song, I begin these acknowledgements.

In many ways, *Everywhere Holy* is a tapestry of experiences and people who have made it possible as I've lived it. I'm a reader and I've read often, so I'm grateful for all the writers before me whose words have inspired and encouraged me and for the fellow writers now who cheer me on, both on and off the page. It's pretty difficult, then, to thank everyone individually who has played a part in the making of this book, but I'll try.

Thank you to my husband, Mike, for loving me like he always has and for holding me to my dreams. I'd never have written this book if he would have indulged my idea to quit on it. The life we've built is a beautiful one—not picture perfect and often chaotic (our circus!)—but it's one we've built together, from scratch, and I'm proud of how we've grown together, just taking one step toward one another each day instead of away. Mike's loyalty is fierce and I'm grateful to have it.

My complete gratitude to my son, Matt. He is the biggest supporter of my writing and the soul friend son I'm so lucky to have. Becoming his mother started an undoing and a remembering and I'm more grateful than I could ever say. He truly is a gift from the other side and I'm very lucky to be the mother of this old soul with the compassionate, empathetic heart.

Thank you to my daughter, Maggie. She is my muse, my rescue, and the daughter I dreamed of and named when I was 16. When she was born, she turned my life upside down, in the best way. Her spirit is strong and light and I'm stronger and lighter simply by her presence. God knew exactly what I needed when he sent this child who loves butterflies to me.

I'm thankful to my parents, Ray and Donna, for many, many things. They have always shown me that the only way through is to keep walking, even when it's really hard, and they've walked with me. They've helped me so much with the kids over the years and while I wrote this book. Simply put: my family is lucky to have them.

To my people, the tried and the true, who span a wide breadth of time and space, and are friends and family alike, my gratitude. You know who you are and you are many, including but not at all limited to my siblings, Kelly and Ray; my nieces and nephews; my grandparents, who have walked with me in the land of the living and even beyond; my aunts; my cousins. And to the ones in the here and now who lift me up on a daily basis, simply *too many to name*, thank you. I have been blessed with a loving family and good friends over the course of my life. Thank you *all* for reminding me at all different stages of my life that yes, I'm enough, *just as I am*. I hope this book holds your hand, as you've done with mine in real life.

Thank you to the school where I spend my days teaching twelfth-grade English, and specifically to Gina, for giving me the flexibility to combine all the things I consider my vocations: mothering, teaching, and writing.

A special thank you to my readers on www.karalawler. com. Who would've known that the little blog I started in 2015 as *Mothering the Divide* would turn into this? Thank you for your love and support. We've truly built an amazing community together. I've been so grateful for our virtual friendship and I still dream of us all in the same room. For now, thank you for showing up on my pages and in my groups. I'll continue to see you there.

I'm so grateful for all of the people who helped bring

this book to life. My gratitude to Blythe Daniel, my agent, who loved my writing from the beginning. Thank you to all of the people over at Harper Collins Christian and Thomas Nelson/Nelson Books, especially Jenny Baumgartner, a true kindred-spirit. She took a chance on me and has been an endless fount of encouragement from day one. Thanks, too, to Brigitta Nortker, Sara Broun, Rachel Tockstein, Aryn VanDyke, and the entire editing and marketing team. Thank you for all you've done to walk with me through all of this and helping me navigate the things that were hard for me, as my first response is usually fear instead of excitement. I'm grateful. And, to those who wrote endorsements and who have offered support in sharing the book with the world, I hope someday I can return the favor.

Finally, and *especially* to the "invisible natures," I would never have written this book without them.

Notes

Introduction
1. Lucy Maud Montgomery, *Anne of Green Gables* (Boston: L. C. Page & Company, 1908), 72.

Chapter 2: Oh, the Rainbows in the Sky
1. Gen. 9:13.
2. Toni Morrison, *Beloved* (New York: Alfred A. Knopf, 1987; New York: Vintage, 2004), 237.
3. Henry David Thoreau, *Walden* (Boston: Houghton, Mifflin & Company, 1882), 304.

Chapter 5: They, So Fresh from God
1. Charles Dickens, *Old Curiosity Shop* (New York: Hurd and Houghton: 1870), 13.

Chapter 10: And the Rain Falls
1. Raymond Lawler Sr., "Rain," 2017. The poem was a gift to the author from her father and reprinted here with permission.

Chapter 11: Angels on Guard

1. Thomas Burnet, *Archaeologiae Philosophicae* (London: Kettilby, 1692), quoted in Samuel Taylor Coleridge, "The Rime of the Ancient Mariner," *Sibylline Leaves* (London: Rest Fenner, 1817), 2.

Chapter 12: The World Within

1. Parker J. Palmer, from a personal conversation with Mark Nepo, quoted in *The Book of Awakening: Having the Life You Want by Being Present to the Life You Have* (York Beach, ME: Red Wheel/Weiser, 2000), 119.
2. Brené Brown, *The Gifts of Imperfection* (Center City, MN: Hazelden Publishing, 2010).
3. Kate Chopin, *The Awakening* (New York: Herbert S. Stone & Company, 1899), 148.

Chapter 13: Life Less Difficult

1. Nepo, *The Book of Awakening*, 198.
2. Paulo Coelho, introduction to *The Alchemist* (San Francisco: HarperSanFrancisco, 2002).
3. Traditional, text online at "Peace Prayer of Saint Francis," Loyola Press, https://www.loyolapress.com/our-catholic-faith/prayer/traditional-catholic-prayers/saints-prayers/peace-prayer-of-saint-francis.

Chapter 14: A Language Without Words

1. "Finding God in All Things," Ignatian Spirituality, accessed March 26, 2019, https://jesuits.org/spirituality.

About the Author

Kara Lawler is a popular writer and blogger whose work has appeared in various publications, including *Today Parents*, *Parenting*, and *HuffPost* and some of her essays have been read millions of times. She holds a BA in English and an MA in education and have been teaching high school English for close to two decades. Kara lives in the Allegheny Mountains of Pennsylvania with her husband of seventeen years, Mike, their two children, Matt and Maggie, two goldendoodles, Frances and Finnegan (a new addition!), two cats, Mary and Lily, a bunny, Sugar, a feisty rooster, Henry, and all his girls including her favorite hens, Henrietta, Sweetie, and Marigold, and a growing brood of ducks and other animals. Kara loves time spent in nature, as she always finds herself and God there amidst the trees. Find Kara on www.karalawler.com or on Facebook.